Praise for Centering Prayer

"Most of us sort out life's problems using words and logic. Brian Russell shows us a better way—to begin from our divinely designed center of gravity: prayer. The best way to experience 'lavish love' and pay it forward is to pray (and play) it forward. This book could change your life."
—**Leonard Sweet,** best-selling author, preacher, and educator

"We live in a crazy world, where people are stressed and burning out. Spiritual burnout occurs when we don't give ourselves time to stop and rest from our busy routine. More than ever, we need to recenter our lives on Christ. More specifically, we need to rediscover the practice of centering prayer that will help sustain us. *Centering Prayer* is a timely book. Read it and you will be refreshed, renewed, and recentered in the presence of God."
—**Dr. Winfield Bevins**, Director of Church Planting at Asbury Seminary and author of *Ever Ancient Ever New*

"Brian Russell shares his story of moving from intellectual assent to heartfelt experience of being loved by God. How did that transformation happen? Read this book to find out for yourself, and you too might discover the beauty of sitting in silence before the One who knows you completely and loves you deeply."
—**Virginia Todd Holeman, PhD, LPCC,** Professor of Counseling, Asbury Theological Seminary

"Soon enough, none of us will remember life before the internet. Our online technologies will have become a kind of foundational myth. Something essential will be missing from our lives, something our ancestors took entirely for granted—an ability to be absent. Whether you are leading in the marketplace or the Church, *Centering Prayer* offers you timeless practices that will help you foster a spirituality that is not just another connection but is the connection to grow in your love of God, neighbor, and yourself."
—**Dr. Mark Dunwoody**, Co-Founder of Missional Formation Coaching and author of *Healthy Rhythms for Leaders*

"Brian Russell invites us to recenter ourselves in God's loving presence through centering prayer. As a gifted teacher and experienced practitioner, Brian is a trustworthy guide for anyone who thirsts, not only to know more about God, but to be with God and walk in his way of love every day."

—Alastair Sterne, lead pastor of St. Peter's Fireside in Vancouver, British Columbia, and author of *Rhythms for Life*

"Russell gives a very down-to-earth, practical presentation of centering prayer and how it can help us grow in the spiritual journey. In particular, he shows how beautifully it reflects the Scriptures and how it can open us up to the healing power of God's Spirit, as experienced through silence. I think this is a very useful read for anyone trying to grow in the spirit."

—Rev. Dr. Murchadh Ó Madagáin, author of *Centering Prayer and the Healing of the Unconscious*

"The loss of prayer in the Christian church is not due to lack of time. We binge-watch Netflix with immense efficiency. It is due to a deep conviction. We think we're better at things than God. Brian Russell invites us not to a new way, but the old way, which is laced with patience and quiet, hope and love, yearning and hoping. Highly recommended."

—A. J. Swoboda, assistant professor of Bible, theology, and World Christianity at Bushnell University and the author of *After Doubt*

"Brian has been to the desert of a fullblown spiritual and emotional crisis, and he knows the way through. The practice of centering prayer has been a sustaining force in his life, and now he shares deep insights from his own growth and failures. This is more than a book—it is a pathway into the transformative love of God."

—Rev. Dr. Michael Adam Beck, author and Director of the Fresh Expressions House of Studies at United Theological Seminary

"Dr. Brian Russell's book is an indispensable guide to discovering the depths of God's love, who we are, and how we're created to live."

—John Carroll, Director of the School of Kingdom Living, Dallas Willard Ministries

CenteringPrayer

Sitting Quietly in God's Presence
Can Change Your Life

BRIAN D. RUSSELL

PARACLETE PRESS
BREWSTER, MASSACHUSETTS

2021 First Printing

Centering Prayer: Sitting Quietly in God's Presence Can Change Your Life

Copyright © 2021 by Brian D. Russell

ISBN 978-1-64060-643-2

Library of Congress Cataloging-in-Publication Data
Names: Russell, Brian D., 1969- author.
Title: Centering prayer : sitting quietly in God's presence can change your life / Brian D. Russell.
Description: Brewster, Massachusetts : Paraclete Press, 2021. | Summary: "How centering prayer can enrich your soul and help you experience God's transforming love"-- Provided by publisher.
Identifiers: LCCN 2021015023 (print) | LCCN 2021015024 (ebook) | ISBN 9781640606432 | ISBN 9781640606449 (epub) | ISBN 9781640606456 (pdf)
Subjects: LCSH: Contemplation. | Prayer--Christianity. | BISAC: RELIGION / Christian Living / Prayer | RELIGION / Christian Living / Spiritual Growth
Classification: LCC BV5091.C7 R87 2021 (print) | LCC BV5091.C7 (ebook) | DDC 248.3/2--dc23
LC record available at https://lccn.loc.gov/2021015023
LC ebook record available at https://lccn.loc.gov/2021015024

10 9 8 7 6 5 4 3 2 1

Published by Paraclete Press
Brewster, Massachusetts
www.paracletepress.com

Printed in the United States of America

CONTENTS

PROLOGUE

God moves toward us on a mission of love.

We love because God first loved us. John 3:16 famously states, "For God so loved the world that he gave his only Son, so that everyone who believes in him may not perish but may have eternal life." Through the Holy Spirit, God's love is poured out into our hearts (Rom. 5:5). This is the heart of the good news. God invites us to serve as witnesses and embodiments of God's love to the world.

I don't know about you, but I've struggled living out this vision consistently. I've come to the conclusion that the root of the problem is deeper than my conscious thoughts about God. As a trained theologian and pastor, I can articulate Christian doctrine well. I've read Scripture consistently now for over thirty-five years. I've preached hundreds of sermons. I've taught biblical studies for over twenty years at the graduate level. I've spoken at dozens of churches, conferences, and camps on topics related to the interpretation of Scripture.

But for too long the God I've worshiped has been more a construct in my mind than the lover of my soul and the object of my own soul's affection. I'm not confessing the harboring of some heretical belief. I'm not suggesting that I've lived in rebellion against God. I'm simply sharing the growing edge of my spiritual life. As I've grown in grace in recent years, I've experienced new depths of God's love for me. Sensing God's love for me has been so transformational that it almost feels as though I've experienced conversion all over again. At the center of this has been my now daily practice of centering prayer.

Centering prayer has enriched my soul. I offer what follows as a testimony and offering to fellow pilgrims on the journey of faith. Most of this book was written following time spent in silence and solitude with God. Centering prayer is part of a morning ritual that prepares me for the abundance of each day. I hope that my experiences and reflections on centering prayer will help you to develop your own practice. Most importantly, I pray that you will deepen your walk with the God who loves you.

I wish that I'd learned of centering prayer earlier in life. Since I've committed to being present with God in the prayer of silence, I've experienced a tangible calming effect. I am less reactive. I'm less anxious. Past wounds weigh me down less. I am a better listener in the presence of others. Most significantly, I've sensed God's love for the world and for me more profoundly. The experience of being deeply loved by God has changed me.

This is a book about transformation. When we truly experience God's love at the core of our being, we are liberated to love God, love others, and even to love ourselves. My goal is to help you on your own personal journey to love.

INTRODUCTION

"I think, therefore I am."
—DESCARTES

I lived most of my life by Descartes's words.

Spending hours thinking propelled me into a career as a professor and thought leader. As many things in life go, this approach worked until it suddenly didn't.

I want to share the story of why I adopted a consistent meditation practice into my life. I'm a practitioner of centering prayer.

There are many forms of meditation. Centering prayer finds its roots in the Christian tradition. The intentional practice of solitude and silence among Christians traces its origins to at least the fourth century, to the beginnings of the monastic movement. By this I mean the large-scale intentional practice of silence and solitude. Jesus withdrew into the wilderness before his public ministry, and the Gospels record him frequently moving away from the crowds for times of prayer. In the fourth century, men and women withdrew into the deserts of Egypt and Syria to seek a deeper level of spirituality. These early adopters formed communities that eventually built monasteries and orders that exist to this day.

Centering prayer arrived at a critical time in my life. A twenty-year marriage had just ended. The accompanying fear and anxiety felt overwhelming. I experienced profound loss at almost every level.

The tipping point arrived after a brief exchange with a concerned friend: "Brian, you are sounding crazy. Are you okay?"

I clearly wasn't. My anxiety had reached such a level that I was talking incessantly and incoherently. I had hit the proverbial "wall." My ability to think clearly had departed. I was not facing an intellectual problem. I was in a full blown emotional and spiritual crisis. I was also facing financial and relational ruin.

My friend's concern served as a wake-up call. I immediately went outside for a walk. I live in Orlando, Florida. It's typically sunny here, and this particular day did not disappoint. There is something restorative about the beauty of Florida's blue sky and sunshine. It was also springtime. The sun's rays felt warm on my skin. I walked several miles that day. I can remember breathing in the fresh air and smelling the fragrance of blossoming flowers. I also recall noticing the stillness of the day and the stunning brightness of the leaves on the trees and shrubbery as I walked. I heard the singing of birds and the buzzing of busy insects.

I thought, "I don't believe I've ever noticed the sheer beauty of the world around me in quite this way."

I realized that I'd walked these paths before but had been blind to the lush scenery. What was different that day? I had left my iPod at home, so I was not listening to music or a podcast. I had what I can only describe as a "God-moment." The sound of a bird captured my attention and caused me to look up and find its perch. My thoughts stilled. I experienced a true sense of presence. I stopped walking and took in my surroundings. It was as though my world shifted from black-and-white to color.

I sensed God's love for me in a way that was new. I wasn't in a worship service. I wasn't studying Scripture. I wasn't trying to perceive God with my intellect. I wasn't engaged in theological reflection. I wasn't celebrating the Lord's Supper. I wasn't praying with words.

I was just fully present, and I felt God's love. I sensed that God was enough, and that there was an abundance of love available for me and for the whole world. Moreover, despite the pain in my life, I became aware that I was enough for God. Theologian Paul Tillich once described the experience of grace this way: "Simply accept the fact that you're accepted."[1]

My experience with God that day was a transformative moment. My life did not instantly get better. I still had the work of caring for my two daughters, grieving my losses, and doing the inner work of healing the wounds that I carried. But that momentary glimpse of God's love changed me. I saw that a deeper level of spirituality was possible. I sensed the presence of God's love in Christ in the midst of the swirling insecurity and uncertainty of a difficult season in my life.

I now recognize that moment as my crash-course introduction to solitude and silence with God. The grace of God astonished me that day and gave me a true taste of divine love. This chance experience grew into my now daily practice of centering prayer. Centering prayer nourishes my soul so that I can live as an ambassador of God's abundant love.

God's love is the essence of this book. Centering prayer is merely a means of opening one's true self to God's love.

I've learned that there are three *loves*. Each calls for expression from us. All love finds its roots in the love of God for us and the world through Jesus Christ by the power of the Spirit. Because God loves us, we respond with love for God, for neighbor, and for ourselves. Love begets love. These three loves swirl together ever more profoundly to do the transformational work of God in our lives.

My prior theological training had not prepared me for this experience. But I've since learned about the Christian contemplative tradition from works by Thomas Merton, Thomas Keating, Cynthia Bourgeault, Richard Rohr, and Murchadh Ó Madagáin, among others. They taught me about centering prayer and rooted it in early and medieval Christian practices. I've now also learned from the early desert fathers such as Antony and Evagrius Ponticus, reflected on the wisdom of Augustine and other Church Fathers, and listened intently to medieval mystics such as Teresa of Avila, Bernard of Clairvaux, and the anonymous author of *The Cloud of Unknowing*. As a trained biblical scholar, I've attempted to interact with Scripture not as a means of "proof texting" centering prayer but to gain new insights into the words of the biblical authors. I've also studied modern authors who've reflected on the spiritual task of the inner healing of our *shadow* persona and *false self*.

Most importantly, I've been practicing silence before God. I say this because centering prayer is a practice. I offer this book not to *teach* you thoughts and ideas about centering prayer, but to equip and empower you to *practice* it as a means to growing in love for God, neighbor, and self.

I offer the following reflections with the hope that I can point fellow pilgrims to the next step of their journey in the lavishness of God's love.

I don't promise you a quick fix. Growth in grace takes a lifetime. Healing rarely happens instantaneously. But a decision to explore new spiritual practices can be made in a moment. God's love may then propel you back into the world to embody and share God's love, grace, mercy, and peace.

PART ONE

How to Practice Centering Prayer

CHAPTER 1

What Centering Prayer Is

"[A]t the beginning of the time of prayer
one simply declares to God your desire to sit in his loving presence
and during your practice you seek to honor this intention."

—JAMES WILHOIT[2]

The practice of centering prayer is simple

to describe but not necessarily easy to implement. Please commit
to experimenting with centering prayer. This book will not be
very helpful to you *unless* you spend time in the practice itself. Your
mind may be able to conceive of the ideas, but centering prayer is
for the whole person. My hope is for you to begin a contemplative
practice or to deepen your current one.

Before introducing the actual method, I want to offer a
description of it.

Centering prayer is first and foremost a method of prayer. As
such, its goal is communion with God. It helps to draw us closer to
God. It deepens our relationship with God. Unlike more common
types of prayer, centering prayer is *wordless* and practiced in *silence*
and most often in *solitude.*[3]

Moreover, centering prayer is a distinctively Christian form of
meditative prayer. At its core, centering prayer involves sitting in
silence with God and *surrendering* or *disengaging* from our thoughts
and feelings. It does not involve using a mantra, exclusively
focusing on our breath, reflecting on an image, or paying attention
to a particular thought. Centering prayer is about opening
ourselves to the work of the Holy Spirit in ways that transcend

our thoughts and feelings. It is preparation for the gift of God's presence in which one may experience love and grace apart from words, thoughts, images, and feelings.

Objectless Awareness

The surrender of our thoughts to God is our sole contribution to the experience of centering prayer.[4] Surrender sets our intention to be silent in the hope of experiencing God's presence. There is no other action that we take. Communion with God is always God's gift to us. We cannot force God to act. Instead, the result of the surrender of thoughts and feelings is the creation of brief spaces or gaps within our thought stream.

What happens when we surrender our attention to our thoughts and feelings? In these moments when we are not focused on anything, we may find ourselves in a place of being that Bourgeault describes as "objectless awareness."[5] Some may find alternative words such as "communion," "oneness," or "is-ness" to be more helpful. Our time in such a space is momentary. In fact, the second we think, "Wow—I'm experiencing oneness with God," we are probably back inside of our thoughts.

The phrase "objectless awareness" may sound mystical or even fanciful. It is not a description of God, but about a space of silence in which one may encounter God beyond our words and emotional capacity to describe. Jones describes it as an experience of "vast inner emptiness."[6]

If all this does not make sense or resonate with you yet, please continue reading. Keep it in the back of your mind and see if it helps over time. The challenge here is that I am attempting to capture in words an *experience* of *consciousness* that is beyond our words, thoughts, and emotions. The more we practice centering prayer the more these descriptive phrases will resonate with our experience of God.

Entering into "objectless awareness" is not about dissolving into the Divine or losing our identity as an individual created being. It is about embracing the silence as a new way of perceiving or experiencing consciousness. We are no longer "seeing" through the lens of a subject pondering some object. Instead, we exist in these moments in a space of silence in which we may experience our truest self being fully known by God.

By "truest self," I mean the sum total of who we are including what some call the false self and shadow persona. In the silence, we are "naked" before God. Nowhere to hide. Nowhere to run. As we will see as we move forward in this book, the experience of true silence is transformational and critical for growing into ever-deepening capacities to love God, love neighbor, and love ourselves.

Yet at the same time, God is not an object of our attention. We and God simply "are." We may experience an awareness that is different from our normal ways of relating. I use the phrase *may experience* because our time of centering prayer does not in any way manipulate or control God. This awareness will not be merely the perception of God as object. God will not automatically engage us in the silence. God's presence is always a gift that we receive without expectation, agenda, or control.

The Cloud of Unknowing and the Cloud of Forgetting

Perhaps you have heard of *The Cloud of Unknowing*. This medieval text offers a visual metaphor of two clouds that may help to make more concrete this idea of "objectless awareness."[7] The product of an anonymous fourteenth-century English mystic,

The Cloud of Unknowing was the primary Christian source material used by Catholic monks Thomas Keating, Basil Pennington, and William Meninger at the beginning of the centering prayer movement about fifty years ago.[8]

When we sit in silence before God, we may find ourselves on the border of a cloud of unknowing. This borderland is a space of darkness from which one "peers" into the cloud of unknowing.[9] From the author of the *Cloud of Unknowing*'s perspective, it exists spatially above us. This is the metaphorical way that the author describes the reality of "objectless awareness." This cloud is what is between us and God. To reach this space involves us rising above a second cloud called "the cloud of forgetting."[10] This second cloud separates us from the rest of created reality. The cloud of forgetting gathers shape through the surrender of our attention to our thoughts, feelings, emotions, memories, and ideas in favor of setting our *intention* to sit in silence before God. We will explore impediments to this boundary space in Part Three. There is no "cloud of unknowing" or "oneness" or "is-ness" or "objectless awareness" unless we are floating above this "cloud of forgetting." Whenever we slide back into our thoughts, we are out of the space in which we can bask even momentarily in the fullness of God's presence. We reach the space above "the cloud of forgetting" via surrender.

Preparation for God's Loving Presence

Centering prayer is a practice that prepares us for the possibility of a dynamic encounter with the Divine in a space or way of being outside our rational thoughts or sensory emotions. Centering prayer takes us to the doorway of God's presence but no further. It is not a means of forcing our way into the house of God's presence.[11] The practice of preparation through the surrender of our thoughts is the human side of centering prayer. This activity shapes us into the types of people who become deeply aware of the reality of God's loving presence. Then, when we find ourselves in the space or way of being between the two clouds, we may experience the gift of God's presence and then begin to embody it as a way of life as we reenter our regular life.

My teacher in spiritual direction, Gene Yotka of the Awakening Institute, offers this insight:

> Centering prayer is a method of prayer which prepares us to receive the gift of God's presence as we enter into divine silence from which we can respond to the Holy Spirit who helps us to surrender to God's presence and action within. This is a conversation initiated by God in which the Lord blesses us with the ability to receive, relate and respond as we grow more and more aware of the Lord's Divine presence in every moment of our lives.[12]

The fruit, then, is more than individual experience. It is growth in grace into the person that God created each of us to be. This growth manifests into all of life and impacts how we live in the world. It shapes how we engage others in the love of Jesus Christ through the power of the Spirit to the glory of God the Father.[13]

The Practice of Centering Prayer

Now that we've offered a definition and discussion of the meaning of centering prayer, let's move to describing the actual practice of it.

Schedule a Time

You can be spontaneous and do centering prayer any time you desire. However, establishing a deep practice usually takes intentional planning. I include a time of centering prayer in my morning routine. On the days I work at home or on weekends, I practice centering prayer at the end of a morning walk. It flows naturally out of time in nature. On days when I work in my office, I arrive thirty minutes early and begin my workday with it. In both cases, this time with God prepares me for the rest of the day.

More advanced practitioners will often schedule multiple sessions. I have friends who bookend their days with a twenty- to twenty-five-minute session in the morning and before bedtime. If you have a family, centering prayer is an excellent way to transition from your work life to your family time. Upon arriving home from work, retreat quickly to a quiet place and sit in silence with God.

Choose the Duration

Those who live a life of solitude such as a monk in a monastery may have the luxury of spending frequent scheduled times in deep contemplation. But for most of us, teachers of centering prayer recommend setting a timer for about twenty minutes. Choose vibrate or a pleasant tone so that the alarm doesn't jar you.

If you are new to the practice, you may want to start with three to five minutes in the morning or evening. Be patient with yourself. The practice of centering prayer is a journey. It is an abiding with God. It is not a competition or a task. If even this seems too much, try one or two minutes. I'm serious. When I first began practicing, even sitting for five minutes was agonizing. It felt as though it lasted an hour! Allow yourself to build up over time.

Do not become legalistic about the duration. Allow it to fit into your life. It is better to have an abbreviated session on a busy day than no session at all. It is likewise a blessing to extend to a half hour or even longer when you can.

Whatever time you choose, do your best to honor your intention. Don't make it a habit to end a session early because you are struggling with your thoughts. There is likely a lesson for you in the struggle.

Create the Atmosphere

Find a quiet and comfortable place where you can sit and maintain good posture. Experiment until you find what works for you. I've sat on a yoga mat cross-legged. I've also used a meditation pillow (yes, you can actually buy such a thing!). Lately, I settled on sitting in a comfy chair with armrests.

My favorite place to practice centering prayer is on my back patio. It faces toward a small retention pond and offers a backdrop of tranquility. When I can't be outside, I find a quiet place indoors where I won't be disturbed.

If you appreciate the senses, burn a candle or incense to enhance the experience. If you are in a space with distracting sounds, try playing some soft instrumental music in the background.

Close Your Eyes

Close your eyes and take a few deep cleansing breaths as a means of shifting from the busyness of the world to your time with God. Remember: centering prayer is nothing more and nothing less than sitting in silence with the intention of being in the presence of the God who loves you.

Set Your Intention

Begin with a prayer such as "Come Lord Jesus." I personally recommend using the Jesus Prayer: "Lord Jesus Christ, Son of God, have mercy on me, a sinner."

The Jesus Prayer goes back into the formative centuries of the early church, and it's rooted in Scripture. You may recognize the phrase "have mercy on me, a sinner" as the words of the tax collector's prayer in Luke 18:13. The Jesus Prayer includes our admission of our need for grace. It is an invitation for the Risen Christ to engage you. This is the core assumption of centering prayer. We are not merely turning inward. We are sitting in silence before God as a means of opening ourselves to communion and connection with our Lord.

Sit Silently and Use a Prayer Word to Break Your Cycles of Thought

Centering prayer involves sitting with our eyes closed in silence before God. There are no work or conscious prayers involved.

Thoughts and images will continually run through our minds. This is normal. The practice of centering prayer turns on our response to the perception of our thoughts. Whenever we find ourselves lost in thought, we use a prayer word to return to the silence and sit before God. Centering prayer is the practice of our ongoing commitment to surrender all thoughts, images, perceptions, and feelings. It is not about locking our attention.

The prayer word (or sacred word) should be a one- or two-syllable word. It is not a mantra that we repeat endlessly. In certain Eastern forms of meditation, a mantra is repeated continuously as a means of breaking our thought stream. Our prayer word is different. It may be repeated multiple times during our prayer session, but unlike a mantra, it is a means of returning to God rather than a point of focus apart from our thoughts. In other words, it is more of a vehicle that represents our intention to be with God. I recommend using "Jesus." After all, Jesus is the object of the prayer. Others, however, may find words such as "faith," "hope," "love," and "Lord" helpful. The key is to select a short word that allows you to gently pull yourself out of your thought loops. When I become conscious of my thoughts, I silently say, "Jesus." This pulls me out of my hamster-wheel mind and brings me back to the space of silence before God. This is the space above the "cloud of forgetting" and just below the "cloud of unknowing." Ó Madagáin helpfully describes the sacred word as an abbreviated form of a prayer of intention.[14] Using a sacred word affirms our desire to surrender fully to God's presence and invites God to work in us.

My colleague Steve Stratton recently shared with me a helpful illustration from the Gospel. Recall the famous scene in which Jesus surprised his disciples by walking on water. Peter desired to join him, and Jesus invited him to step out upon the waters. As Peter moved out of the boat and onto the sea, he hesitated and lost focus. Rather than keeping his eyes on Jesus, he turned his vision to the wind. This caused him to sink. As he slipped into the waters, Peter cried out, "Lord, save me" (Matt. 14:30). Jesus immediately reached out and steadied him. This is the process of centering prayer, and it is why we use a prayer word. It allows us to realign with the true purpose of our silence—preparing ourselves for intimacy with God.

Make No Judgment on Stray Thoughts

The average person has thousands of thoughts every day. Even in a twenty-minute centering prayer session, we will experience an ongoing cascade of thoughts. Go ahead and acknowledge them— you waste time by trying to "push" them away—but then just as simply recenter on Jesus using the sacred word. In Part Three, we will explore the variety of thoughts you will likely encounter.

The Four Rs

The classic advice on managing our stream of thoughts in centering prayer is this:

Resist no thought.
Retain no thought.
React to no thought.
Return ever so gently to the sacred word.[15]

These "Four Rs" are full of wisdom. They assist us in operationalizing the core principles of centering prayer—the surrender of our thoughts and our return to the intention to sit in silence before God. We cannot control our thoughts. They may be beautiful; they may be embarrassing; they may be random. Regardless, when we recognize that they've grabbed our attention, we release them and return to the silence with our sacred word.

Resist no thought. Recognize that we spend most of our days lost in loops of thought. Our minds bounce endlessly from one thought to another. Buddhists call this the "monkey mind." To practice centering prayer does not mean fighting against thinking. The goal is not to erase our minds. This is impossible. You will likely have hundreds of thoughts during a centering prayer session. The key is recognizing when this happens and then surrendering anew. This leads to the next "R."

Retain no thought. During centering prayer, we release our thoughts whenever we find ourselves paying attention to one. This is easy if it's a random thought about dinner or about a bug buzzing in our ear. However, if we generate a helpful solution to a problem we've struggled with, it is harder to let go. But let go we must. Good or bad or neutral, we surrender each thought and return to the silence.

React to no thought. Thoughts are just thoughts. We have little control of what moves into our conscious mind. We may encounter beautiful thoughts or disturbing ones. A painful memory may emerge from the depths of our soul. We may get caught up in a fantasy. Regardless, the practice of centering prayer involves our commitment to make no judgments regarding our thoughts. Instead, we release them to God.

Return ever so gently to the sacred word. The elegance of centering prayer is its simplicity. It's all about our intention to spend time with God in silence. The sacred word serves as a means of breaking our attention to thoughts, words, images, and feelings so that we can return to the silence.

Repeat this process for the duration of your time. When your timer chimes or vibrates, take a few final breaths and then close with the Lord's Prayer or a prayer of your own.

Closing Advice

(1) Remember the goal of centering prayer is the practice itself. We are not running a race to win the prize of spiritual growth. We are not competing with others. We are not even competing with ourselves. Sitting in silence in the presence of the God who loves us *is* the point.

(2) Centering prayer is not an action to create a spiritual experience. It is not a shortcut to intimacy with God. It *may* indeed lead to deep contemplative experiences with God, but we must not view it as a technique to *control* or *manipulate* God's presence. God's presence is always a gift of grace. Thomas Merton's words are helpful, "No natural exercise can bring

you into vital contact with Him. Unless He utters Himself in you, speaks His own name in the center of your soul, you will no more know Him than a stone knows the ground upon which it rests in its inertia."[16]

(3) If you are interrupted by a phone, a bird, or any sound, don't stress. You may need to open your eyes for a moment or two. If this happens, simply drop back into your session.

(4) Do not judge your results on a few sessions. Commit to staying with the practice for at least thirty days.

(5) As part of your daily rhythm of life, learn to take small one- or two-minute breaks during the day. If you are working, you may find it helpful to slip into your office or a quiet corner of your workspace, or go outside during a break. If you are at home, the need for silence still applies. Close your eyes and allow yourself to recenter your day on Jesus.

And now, before continuing with this book, I invite you to spend time in silence using the above instructions.

CHAPTER 2

Why Our Souls Need Solitude

"In a revealed religion, silence with God has a value in itself and
for its own sake, just because God is God. Failure to recognize
the value of mere being with God, as the beloved, without doing
anything, is to gouge the heart out of Christianity."

—EDWARD SCHILLEBEECKX[17]

Have you ever found yourself attempting to
navigate an unfamiliar area with an old map or with a GPS
system that hasn't been updated? We all know the feeling of being
in a strange place and realizing that the maps at our disposal are
missing key features. I think of the practice of silence and solitude
in centering prayer as a new, more detailed map for my spiritual
growth. But before talking about my new map, let me share with
you my old one.

Maps are fantastic tools for navigating the world until they
aren't. But you only discover the inadequacy of a map when
you find yourself off grid. This happens in times when our map
doesn't match the terrain we find ourselves in. This scenario also
usually manifests at the most challenging or inconvenient times.

My experience of divorce after a twenty-year marriage can
only be described as an inner searing of my soul. It rocked my
previous belief structure to the core. I could not make intellectual,
emotional, or spiritual sense of any of it. I was reduced to being
an anxiety-ridden insomniac whose previous faith commitments

seemed almost a foreign country. My former spiritual maps had many intellectual answers, but these didn't penetrate the pain.

As I look back almost a decade later, I've never returned to the land I once inhabited. But I'm also no longer off grid. My faith and life have expanded in unexpected ways. My spiritual life has become richer and deeper. I am now grateful for the period of personal purgatory caused by the dissolution of my first marriage.

What has been the difference maker for me? It's been my embrace of the habits of silence and solitude. My daily practice of centering prayer sits at the core of these practices. Centering prayer has given me a new map that filled in details that my previous maps left uncharted.

In the introduction, I shared the story of my initial experience of contemplation. I didn't find silence and solitude as much as it found me. It was the gift that served as an anchor when I was slipping and as a trustworthy guide for growing in the love of God, neighbor, and self.

My anxiety-driven brain had kept looping and grasping for answers. But my experience of peace in a moment of contemplation interrupted my thoughts and taught me a critical lesson: *My undisciplined mind was an impediment to my growth in love.* I say "undisciplined," because I want to avoid sounding anti-intellectual or anti-rational. After all, I make my living by thinking.

The truth is that our minds run nonstop. One of the profound steps on the journey to deep communion with God occurs when we recognize the extent to which we are lost in endless thought loops.

Ponder for a moment this idea: *We are not merely our thoughts.* It also seems true that we have little control of the variety of thoughts that flood our minds. If you struggle in accepting this idea, recall random dreams that you have while sleeping. How much influence do you have over the content of your dreams?

We are flesh and bones filled with DNA inherited from our ancestors. Scripture tells us that each of us is also forged in the image of God (Gen. 1:26–31). There are different ways to express the physical and spiritual dimensions of ourselves. I prefer to say that we are "embodied souls." Our conscious thoughts are simply one aspect of our experience of life.

Even more importantly, God is more than, and greater than, any thought or feeling we may ponder or experience. Reflecting on the beauty of God through our tradition merely scratches the surface of the infinite nature of God.

God is richer and deeper than the theology we use to describe our beliefs. For example, St. Anselm in his well-known reflection on the existence of God in his *Proslogium* described God as that which nothing greater can be conceived. Part of Anselm's thinking involved recognizing that the God whom we are capable of imagining and understanding in our minds is radically less than the fullness of who God truly is.

Why is this important? For some it may not be. But there are pilgrims who long for something more tangible than descriptions or depictions of God. They long for deep relationships with God that penetrate our minds, hearts, feelings, and even our physical bodies. In Philippians 3:9–10 Paul wrote of his desire to "be found in [Christ], not having a righteousness of my own that comes from the law, but one that comes through faith in Christ. . . . I want to know Christ and the power of his resurrection." A verse earlier Paul equated the ultimate gain in life—what he called "the surpassing value"—with knowing Christ. This is not merely knowledge that one gains through study. This is deep intimacy that transcends our greatest thoughts and feelings about God.

How Does the Finite Relate to the Infinite?

God's deepest work involves the Holy Spirit working in us at the soul level. Paul hints at this in Romans chapter eight:

> The Spirit himself testifies with our spirit that we are God's children.
>
> In the same way, the Spirit helps us in our weakness. We do not know what we ought to pray for, but the Spirit himself intercedes for us through wordless groans.
>   (Rom. 8:16, 26, NIV)

The experiences that Paul describes do not happen in the world of thoughts, ideas, and feelings. Such encounters occur beyond the noise of our common life. We normally can enter these rich veins of spiritual awakening only in the intentional practices of silence and solitude. These are liminal spaces where our being encounters God's Spirit.

Jungian analyst James Hollis recommends sitting in solitude as a vital practice for engaging our truest self.[18] For Hollis, solitude is a means of confronting the inner noise and chatter that distracts us and hinders us from wholeness. He writes of the need for regular practice:

> So some part of every day, it is good to risk radical presence to oneself, to follow a quiet ritual of disengagement from the traffic out there and the traffic in here. When the silence speaks, one has gained companionship with oneself, moved from loneliness to solitude, a necessary prerequisite to individuation.[19]

According to Hollis, solitude is a path for integrating our lived-out persona (our "false" self) with the shadow that lurks beneath. In Jungian thought, the shadow is more than some evil or dark part of ourselves. There may be elements of our shadow that contain our inner "bad boy" or "bad girl," but there is much more. The shadow is the mirror reflection of our public image. It shows up when no one is watching or when we find ourselves with people whom we trust deeply. We suppress core aspects of ourselves as we mature in order to fit in. Perhaps we loved art or music as a child, but we had parents who discouraged such pursuits. As we matured, we left behind these creative outlets lest we lose the love or approval of father or mother. Hollis suggests that solitude is a vehicle for discovering the true self. Solitude works because it is a way of affirming that our healing cannot depend on another person or thing. The cure for deep loneliness of the soul is solitude rather than the pursuit of distracting relationships.

As Christians, we recognize that only God can truly save us. God's sanctifying grace through the work of the Spirit is the means of experiencing wholeness and approaching an integrated "true self." But the practice of solitude is a way of signaling our dependence on God alone for deep healing. There is of course a place for community. Community is crucial for our spiritual formation. But no one can practice solitude for us or even with us.

Solitude can be frightening. As Nietzsche reminds us, "When we are alone and quiet we are afraid that something will be whispered in our ear, and so we hate the silence and drug ourselves with social life."[20]

Hollis and Nietzsche write from a secular perspective, yet note the high value that each places on solitude and silence. As Christians, we do not engage the silence merely to be alone. We engage the silence as a means of being alone with God. This is a critical distinction. Centering prayer runs much deeper than any solitude or meditation practice that focuses merely on the self. If you practice centering prayer, you will gain deep insight into yourself, but this is a fruit of the practice rather than its purpose.

Centering prayer intends to present our true self fully, openly, and unabashedly to the God who loves us. We will confront our false self and its shadow. In the intimacy of silence with God, we will be touched with the fullness of God's love. This is transformational. Our true self—the person whom God created us to be—begins to emerge out of our times of communion with God. This is part of the deep healing that God works in our souls. As we do this, we will grow in our love for God, for neighbor, and for ourselves. Then we may offer our true, integrated self fully in service to God.

What I'm describing is not easy. Struggling with the false self and its shadow involves facing our inner demons. I'm not suggesting a literal combat with otherworldly forces, but you will face those parts of yourself that you'd otherwise ignore or repress. There will likely be painful and even frightening aspects. How many of us really desire to know the deep recesses of our soul? As Solzhenitsyn wrote, "[T]he line dividing good and evil cuts through the heart of every human being."[21] Yet growth in grace reveals our deepest self and offers us the truth of God's love for even the darkest parts and most painful memories.

Centering prayer serves as a vehicle for surrendering our need to focus on our thoughts. We turn away from them to be present in silence before the God who loves us. We do not give our attention to our thoughts—no matter how beautiful or ugly they may be; rather, we express our intention to spend time with God by surrendering them.[22]

How Does God Work in This Way?

In silence we may experience a purifying new type of conversion. Franciscan Father Richard Rohr uses the language of moral conversion but views it as broader than the overcoming of vices. He writes:

> It is more subtle—a purification of your real motives for doing things (even good things) from the usual desires for personal satisfaction, a need for control personally or socially, or any craving to build up the ego or feel good about yourself. Instead, you shift to the honest perception of value outside yourself.[23]

Solitude, silence, and stillness are all countermeasures to the endless repetitive mind loops that may not serve us in our relationship with God, self, or others. Rohr says:

> I would even say that on the practical level, silence and God will be experienced simultaneously—and even as the same thing. . . . When you are in your mind, you are never truly at peace, and when you are truly at peace you are never in your mind.[24]

Rohr is not denigrating the intellect. It is profoundly helpful to contemplate deeply the beauty and truth of God through words, images, and sounds through thought and emotion. We need the language of Scripture and theology. We need worship songs and hymns of the faith to give voice to our adoration of God. Silence and solitude sit upon the foundation of "the faith that was once for all entrusted to the saints" (Jude 1:3).

We still need careful study of the Bible and theology. Paul Achtemeier, one of my New Testament teachers, used to ask in class, "Since when is ignorance an asset to ministry?" We would all likely agree that it rarely or ever is. Learning is critical, but learning must translate to transformation—especially when the subject is the God who loves us. We shouldn't settle for merely gaining information. Learning must also serve God's bigger mission of manifesting God's kingdom in the world through faith, hope, and love.

The danger of an intellectual approach to faith is equating thoughts *about* God with a moment-by-moment relationship *with* God. When we think about God, God becomes an object—an abstraction in our mind. When we are present with God in deep silence, God is subject. But God is subject without reducing us to mere objects. There is deep relational communion in which we may become lost in God's presence. There is an experience of "oneness" in our spirit with God.

There is even a danger in a book such as this. My goal is not merely to give you ideas to ponder (the *what*), but to empower and inspire you to practice centering prayer daily (the *how*). If I do the former, but not the latter, I've failed. By overfocusing on the intellect, apart from practice, we raise information and facts onto a pedestal. In fact, the brilliance of some scholars may ironically cause ordinary Christians to lose access to the reality of the Divine. Peter Rollins writes:

> In this way Christianity is given over to the scholar who sits at her desk, surrounded on all sides by an endless sea of ink, adding her own tiny drops so as to justify her living. The truth of Christianity is thus given over to those who can dissect it, study it, and reflect upon it.[25]

When God becomes an object of study, we risk creating an idol of our theological reflection.

Part of the reason my initial map failed in a moment of crisis was that I'd focused on viewing faith as an intellectual problem. If I could just learn how to think and frame challenges and issues theologically, I'd be able to work them out and live faithfully. The deep sense of personal betrayal and shame that I felt from my divorce, as well as the struggle to care for my young daughters as a single father, had no place on my old map. I was so hurt that when I attended worship I could not bring myself to sing hymns or praise songs. There was no advice any of my theological mentors could give that gave me any comfort. Even reading Scripture did little to soothe my wound. I didn't need more information. I needed God. Thanks be to God that I stumbled into silence!

Now, sit in silence with the Lord. Resist no thought. Retain no thought. React to no thought. Return ever so gently to the sacred word.

CHAPTER 3

How to Fail at Centering Prayer

"Taste and see that the LORD is good;
happy are those who take refuge in him."

—PSALM 34:8

Centering prayer is a posture of conscious

surrender in which we sit in silence, offering ourselves to God, and inviting God into that space. But we cannot force God to act in a certain way. In chapters 3–8, I want to offer a series of reflections based on my personal practice as well as from testimonies of persons close to me. In the process, I will draw out insights from Scripture to provide biblical images and ideas for thinking about the practice of solitude in centering prayer.

I again want to caution you against reading what follows as a blow-by-blow account of what you will encounter. I cannot promise five steps to the abundant life or thirty days to personal renewal. Centering prayer is not a quick fix, nor should we approach it as a trendy spiritual practice. We simply sit in silence and await the Lord's presence in the spirit of the psalmist: "As a deer longs for flowing streams, so my soul longs for you, O God" (Ps. 42:1).

When I introduce students to the practice of centering prayer, I warn them about being overwhelmed by their thoughts. That is, if they can even step outside of their minds for a few moments to notice themselves lost in thought. Yet many beginners feel as though they are failures. This is far from the truth. One only "fails" at centering prayer by not practicing.

Even if you set the intention to surrender thoughts to God but end up lost in them, you still turned to God one time. If you consider it a failure that you had to use your prayer word dozens or hundreds of times, you are likewise missing an important insight. You are on the journey. You are on the road to awareness and a less distracted presence before God.

Failing at centering prayer is in fact the way to "win." It's part of the learning process of dying to my right to my thoughts. Using my prayer word a hundred times in a twenty-minute session is the equivalent of one hundred push-ups or sit-ups in the gym. Multiple reps of exercises are good for our bodies. Likewise realigning with God through the surrender of our thoughts is good for our minds and souls. It builds resilience and prepares us for life during the remainder of our waking hours. It slowly teaches us the process of what Paul meant when he said, "we take every thought captive to obey Christ" (2 Cor. 10:5).

We are learning to practice the presence of God.

What does this look like on the ground? Let me share some concrete examples. If a driver cuts me off in traffic, I may begin to react angrily. But sometimes I am able to recognize my thoughts and release them. Then I don't brood or ruminate about that driver for minutes or hours.

In meetings, when I catch myself distracted by a daydream or thinking about checking my email, I surrender the desire and return my attention to the actual meeting.

When I am writing in the morning, I may suddenly feel the pull of social media. But instead of leaving my word processor for the web, I recenter on the work of writing.

When I'm speaking with a friend and find myself waiting for him or her to finish so that I can talk, I let go and refocus on listening attentively.

When I am making love to my wife and become overly focused on my own pleasure or am distracted by a stray thought about work or some stressor in my life, I realign with her eyes, match her breathing and enjoy the deep loving intimacy we share.

When I'm standing in line waiting to check out at the grocery store and discover myself unconsciously reaching for my smartphone, I bring my hands into a quiet posture of prayer and enjoy the opportunity to chill and wait for my turn.

When I'm tired and driving in heavy, slow traffic and begin to feel frustration bubbling to the surface, I take a deep breath and surrender.

I share the above as words of encouragement. Believe me, there are still plenty of times when I fail at being present. I am still growing in my consistency, but I'm seeing slow progress. But also remember: *We are not robots*. It is likely impossible to lock into the present moment 24/7 or even for our fifteen to twenty minutes of sitting in silence with our loving Lord.

Yet as the examples above suggest, there is a method in the madness and we slowly grow in grace. God uses our continual realigning with him to shape and form us into people who can do this in the real world. Learning to love God leads to learning to love others. Learning to love others leads to learning to love ourselves.

Now, sit in silence with the Lord. Resist no thought. Retain no thought. React to no thought. Return ever so gently to the sacred word.

CHAPTER 4

Centering Prayer and Loving to Perfection

"Let love well up and stream through us as the beat, pulse,
and rhythm of our lives."
—JAMES OLTHUIS[26]

Centering prayer is a catalyst for growing

in love. We love because God first loved us. Loving God translates
into love for others and love for ourselves. Growing in love actually
increases our capacity for even more love. My sense is that there
is no limit to giving or receiving love. The only impediments
are the blocks (both willful and unconscious) that we establish.
Unfortunately, these self-imposed blocks serve as the ceiling for
our ability to give and receive love.

Think of these blocks as our internal thermostat. At what
temperature is your ability to love set? I ask this because *change*
is possible. What if each of us could simply become ten percent
more loving?

Scripture challenges us to raise the setting on our love
thermostat. Consider Matthew 5:48: "Be perfect, therefore, as
your heavenly Father is perfect." Most of us assume that Jesus
wasn't serious when he said these words. However, the early
church believed it was possible to live out Jesus's command.[27]

Most of us recoil at this thought because we equate *perfection*
with *logical* or *mathematical* perfection. In Matthew's Gospel, it is
perfection in *love*.

In Matthew 5:43–48, Jesus offers God the Father as the model of perfect love. God loves in ways that contrast with typical human expressions of love. In this text, Jesus illustrates perfect love by observing that the Father sends rain on both the righteous and the unrighteous. The implication is this: *God loves indiscriminately.* There are no conditions attached. In contrast, Jesus reminds his listeners of the inconsistency of religious people who model their love on worldly patterns rather than on God's way. In the world, we tend to love those who love us (vv. 46–47). Jesus challenges us to love not as the world does. To love as the world does is the easy way. It is the way of exclusion, judgment, and hypocrisy.

Instead, our model is the Father. In this part of Matthew's Gospel there is a clustering of "father" language used for God.[28] The imagery of God as father emphasizes that love at its core involves relationships as in a healthy family.

This insight reframes the call to "Be perfect" in relational terms. *Perfection* is not mathematical perfection. This connection of perfection with love is critical. As modern women and men, we may indeed shy away from talk of perfection out of the recognition of our many flaws. We recognize the complexity of our inner world. The lesson from the wisdom of the desert mothers and fathers is simple. Their emphasis is love. "To love is human; not to love is less than human."[29] To be perfect in the way of Matthew 5:48 is not a destination but the journey of becoming *more* human in terms of love for God, for others, and for self. It is a continual realignment in light of God's love and the needs of the moment.

Roberta Bondi puts it this way:

Our growing love is a continuous movement into God's love, as the ancient Christian writers say. But because God's love is without limit, and because being human means sharing in the image of God, we can never in our human loving reach the limit of our ability to love. This means that though we may love fully at any one moment, it is not perfect love unless that love continues to grow.[30]

Gregory of Nyssa (a fourth-century theologian) wrote, "For this is truly perfection: never to stop growing towards what is better and never placing any limit on perfection."[31]

Another way of thinking about growth in love is to view it as a journey. We don't ask, "Are we there yet?" or "Will we ever make it?" Instead, we ponder, "How far can we get?" Thus, perfection does not become a fixed point. Perfection becomes a living reality, attitude, and openness to growth.

I find it helpful to ponder the ocean as a metaphor for love. If God's love is the ocean, there are no limits to it.

Imagine your favorite beach. See the sand and watch the waves roll up back and forth. Walk to the water's edge. Feel the wet sand under your feet. This is like your first taste of love. It is inviting. Plus, there is more to experience. So, now dip your toe to test the temperature of the water. Slowly enter the water. As you move into the ocean, it slowly envelops your body. First you are ankle deep, then it rises up to your knees, then waist, then chest, and finally you find yourself literally in over your head. Marvel at the reality that you are probably only a few yards offshore at this point. Most of us stop once we can no longer touch the bottom, yet there is so much more to explore, as the ocean's depths are endless from our finite and limited perspectives as humans.

Growth in love is like exploring the deepest seas. There is always more. Contrast the difference between dipping your toes in at the seashore and descending into the Mariana Trench in the western Pacific Ocean. The maximum known depth in the trench is an area known as Challenger Deep. It is nearly seven miles below the surface! To put this in perspective, you could sink Mount Everest into Challenger Deep and it would be completely submerged with its peak a full 1.2 miles under the surface.

Thus, to be fully immersed in the ocean could mean being a few yards offshore, over one's head, or it could mean being seven miles down in Challenger Deep. Growth in love is God's invitation into God's depths. Once we experience full immersion we have not arrived; we have simply begun an ongoing journey into even greater depths. This in turn expands our capacity to love others and to love ourselves.

The question then is simple: *How deep do we want to go in our growth in love?*

Again, imagine a trip to the beach. Are you content to merely look at the ocean in some detached way from a hotel balcony or from the parking lot? Assuming you are physically able, do you want to move toward the experience of the water itself?

Tasting God's love in centering prayer invites us into deeper and deeper levels.

◯

Now, sit in silence with the Lord. Resist no thought. Retain no thought. React to no thought. Return ever so gently to the sacred word.

CHAPTER 5

Centering Prayer and Meditation

"Silence is God's first language."

—JOHN OF THE CROSS

When I describe centering prayer as an ancient Christian meditation practice, I'm aware how the word *meditation* raises red flags for some who associate meditation with Eastern religions or Western New Age spirituality. Let me address these concerns. More specifically, I'll answer this question: How does centering prayer differ from the types of meditation used in other religions?

The twenty-first century has witnessed a revival of meditation, especially in the Western world. Meditation has been popularized through an emphasis on mindfulness both as a way of inoculation against stress but also as a tool for productivity. Beside mindfulness practices, TM (transcendental meditation) has gained a loyal following among high achievers from billionaire investor Ray Dalio to Arnold Schwarzenegger to influential authors/podcasters such as Tim Ferriss.[32] Of course meditation is core to Eastern religions such as Hinduism and Buddhism. Many have also experienced short, guided meditations at the close of yoga sessions in studios and gyms across the country.

First, it must be acknowledged that centering prayer shares a key element with other meditative traditions—practitioners must be willing to recognize the continuous flow of thoughts within their minds.[33] But this is merely a superficial similarity.

Centering prayer is different from forms of meditation in Eastern religions because of its intention to encounter the living God. It is not simply about emptying our thoughts or experiencing mindfulness in the present moment. The goal is to sit in silence as a means of opening the deepest parts of our being to communion with the God who loves us. If other meditative traditions focus one's attention on the breath, a burning candle, a repetitive mantra, or some part of the body, centering prayer is about one's *intention* to sit with God in silence and surrender whatever thoughts we may encounter. One makes the decision, in Bourgeault's words, to "relinquish attachment to one's surface flow of thoughts and associations, and to rest instead in the undifferentiated presence of God. . . . One might also call it, for reasons that will shortly become clear, the willingness to let go of thoughts as they arise and return to the sacred word as a symbol of one's consent to rest in God."[34]

In other words, centering prayer is a Christian practice because its end goal focuses on the Lord Jesus Christ. Its central aim is the cultivation of a relationship with the God who loves us. The stress on the intention of the centering prayer practitioner is critical. It makes clear that centering prayer is not a work of human achievement through one's deliberate focus or the rapid repetition of a mantra. It is not a technique for self-improvement or self-absorption. Its goal is Christlikeness.[35]

Centering prayer becomes a time of grace. If you need more sources for this, let me point to a few: Wilhoit credits Keating with emphasizing intention over attention. He remarks, "Keating's emphasis on intention allows for a gracious tenor to pervade this prayer practice. It is not a practice of human achievement, but one of intentionality and receptivity."[36] And Bourgeault draws a helpful distinction between the willingness on the part of the practitioner and willfulness.[37] One points to intention and the other to attention. She connects willingness to words such as surrender, openness, and vulnerability. It is the desire to be in God's presence without an agenda. In contrast, willfulness involves control and effort. We attempt to concentrate deeply as a means of escaping thought versus willingly consenting to sit in the presence of God without fighting the thoughts that come to mind.

John Cassian (fifth century) advocated using this prayer sentence from Psalm 70, "Be pleased, O God, to deliver me. O LORD, make haste to help me" (70:1). Reflecting on this verse, Cassian wrote, "It is not without good reason that this verse has been chosen from the whole of Scripture as a device. It carries within it all the feeling of which human nature is capable."[38] Cassian's words help to illustrate the meaning of *intention.*

The beauty of centering prayer is the ongoing intention of open surrender to God. It is not our work. It is similar to the practice of Sabbath. At the heart of Sabbath is the command to do no work. The following words of Waldemar Janzen describe the Sabbath but could easily substitute as a description of centering prayer:

> This is the paradox of grace, that the most important thing humans can do for God is to desist from trying to do anything. . . . The Sabbath is, above all, a call for humans to let God be God and to desist from all human attempts to manage the world through work and achievement, including religious work and achievement.[39]

The goal is neither mindlessness nor a mindfulness detached from our commitment to a relationship with God.

An unfair critique often directed at centering prayer equates it with mindfulness meditation. The underlying criticism implies that centering prayer is more Buddhist than Christian. This is a fundamental misunderstanding. Of course, the practice of centering prayer will over time make practitioners aware of patterns of incessant thought. Like mindfulness meditation, the practice of centering prayer will result in you being more present in life and mindful of the moment, but this is not the goal. Bourgeault writes:

> To be sure practitioners of the prayer do generally experience deep periods of interior quiet, but Keating makes it clear that God is not found in the quiet per se but in the action of consent itself, a consent to whatever emerges.[40]

Thus, it is less about the mind and more the heart. We don't meet God in thought. We encounter God in love. This is an affective movement.

In other words, centering prayer is about focusing on God with our whole being. It is not a mental exercise. We come to God to engage heart to heart. We use our feelings. Bourgeault writes, "By embracing the full intensity of these feelings, an ardor is generated that catapults the heart free and clear of its egocentric orbit and straight into the heart of God."[41]

Our goal is communion with God. Centering prayer is not a technique to create this communion, but a way of being open in order to receive it as God's gift. Our hearts surrender in love before the God who loves us. For this reason, Bourgeault warns against any ego-centered ambitiousness: "But it is important never to lose sight of the fact that spiritual ambitiousness and attention of the heart are mutually exclusive categories. . . . The heart has its built-in safeguard: it perceives only in the modality of surrender."[42]

◯

Now, sit in silence with the Lord. Resist no thought. Retain no thought. React to no thought. Return ever so gently to the sacred word.

CHAPTER 6

Deep Surrender

"The more we get what we call 'ourselves' out of the way and let
God take us over, the more truly ourselves we become."

—C. S. LEWIS

The process of surrender is critical to the

taming of our need for control. When we practice centering
prayer, we commit to sitting in silence with God, and this is a
form of self-denial.

Recall Jesus's summary of the essence of discipleship: "If any
want to become my followers, let them deny themselves and take
up their cross and follow me" (Matt. 16:24, cf. Mark 8:34, Luke
9:27). The focus of discipleship in the Gospels is on *consciously*
following Jesus. Jesus's words may serve as a model for centering
prayer.

In Matthew 16:21, Jesus had laid out the necessity of his
journey to Jerusalem. There Jesus would experience suffering,
death, but also resurrection. In response to this revelation
(16:22), Peter attempted to rebuke Jesus by saying, "God forbid
it, Lord! This must never happen to you." Jesus responded to
Peter with "Get behind me, Satan! You are a stumbling block
to me; for you are setting your mind not on divine things but on
human things" (16:23). In other words, Peter struggled because
he assumed that his plans, desires, and will should govern the
actions of Jesus his Lord.

This is not to say that our goals and ideas have no value.
As we live in the world, we will continually take decisions and

act. But the process of growth in grace involves removing the idolatry and injustice out of our decisions. The challenge of a spiritual life involves learning about the mind of Christ and then discovering that our truest humanity resides in living fully as the person whom God created us to be. The irony is that we are often the greatest impediment to our growth. Our false self attempts to block access to discovering who we are at the deepest level. This was Peter's error.

To set our mind on the things of humanity means that it is our will and talents that remain in control of our destiny. It is the full flourishing of our flesh apart from reliance on the Holy Spirit (see Rom. 8:1–17).

To set our minds on the things of God involves realigning continually with the will of God. Our guide is Jesus. Centering prayer allows us to practice this ongoing surrender of the will.

Matthew 16:24 begins with an invitation: "If any want to become my followers . . ." Jesus calls would-be followers to set an intention. Decide and commit to go in the way of Jesus. Jesus calls us to a relationship with him, the Son of God. When we make the decision to sit in silence, we are answering the call of Jesus.

What does this intention or decision involve? It involves surrender to a new mode of being. In centering prayer, we do not set the agenda. In fact, there is no agenda. The moment we establish one we have gone the way of Peter and set our mind on the ways of humanity.

What does surrender look like? Jesus uses three phrases in 16:24: deny self, take up the cross, and continually follow me.

Deny self. This is not merely a call to a disciplined life involving deprivation. It is more radical. To deny self means to orient fully to the way of Jesus so that the cross shapes our goals, desires, rights, and privileges. In centering prayer, this means a steadfast recognition that my stray thoughts, emotional baggage, and even brilliant insights must give way to being present with God.

Take up the cross. In the ancient world, the cross was a terrifying symbol. Crucifixion was gruesome and humiliating, and it meant certain death. To take up one's cross meant literally lifting the wood upon which one would soon die and walking under its weight to the place of your execution. A person taking up the cross was a dead man or woman walking. In silence, we come to God empty-handed in the surrendered posture of one whose life is over. This frees us from both past and future in order to be with God in the moment.

Continually follow me. If the first two phrases involve letting go of one's rights, privileges, past, and future, Jesus's final phrase points to the pathway for the present. Disciples follow Jesus moment by moment. This was true during Jesus's earthly ministry. It remained true for the Christians to whom Matthew was writing in the first century. Jesus's words are still vital for us today. Discipleship involves a deep, ongoing relationship with Jesus. This is why Jesus came to earth. In Matthew's Gospel, Jesus is Emmanuel, "God with us" (1:23). In Matthew 18:20, Jesus promises, "For where two or three are gathered in my name, I am there among them." In Matthew 28:20, the risen Jesus declares, "And remember, I am with you always, to the end of the age."

In centering prayer, denying self and taking up the cross serve as the means of purging our rights to ourselves. Whatever thoughts, feelings, desires, dreams, goals, visions, triumphant memories, or nightmarish recollections arise during our time of prayer, we surrender them and *continually follow Jesus.* We surrender by recognizing that we are lost in a thought and then using our prayer word to realign ourselves with our Lord.

Imagine yourself taking a walk with Jesus. He leads you down a path. You hear birds singing, so you look up for a moment. You then turn your gaze back to Jesus. Then you get an idea for a project at work, followed by a worry that you don't have enough time to accomplish your goals for the day. You catch yourself and again return to the master. A few moments later you reach a point in the path that triggers a painful memory of great loss. Yet again you turn to Jesus. Martin Luther's dictum comes to mind in this process: "You can't prevent a bird from landing in your tree, but you don't have to allow it to build a nest."

Recognize that the process of centering prayer is to return continually to the Lord. Period. Thoughts are thoughts. Feelings are feelings. Memories are memories. The call to discipleship challenges us to turn away from self and follow Jesus. This is the way of prayer, too. The issue is trust: *Do I trust God enough to release my attachments to whatever the hamster wheel inside my head offers up?*

Thomas Merton writes on the need for continual surrender, "to have a will that is always ready to fold back within itself and draw all the powers of the soul down from its deepest center to rest in silent expectancy for the coming of God, poised in tranquil and effortless concentration upon the point of my dependence on him."[43]

There is a dynamic tension between surrender and our role in the surrender. Merton's words capture it well. It is not that our will disappears. Our will remains. Its intentions, however, are now aligned with the divine will. The Lord's prayer becomes a reality in our inner world, "on earth [in me] as it is in heaven."

In fact, the process of recentering is the critical discipline that opens us up to God's presence and grace. There are no contemplative moments apart from our conscious return to God every time that we find ourselves lost in a stream of thought. This is how souls are made. It is a moment-by-moment journey.

Now, sit in silence with the Lord. Resist no thought. Retain no thought. React to no thought. Return ever so gently to the sacred word.

CHAPTER 7

Centering Prayer
as Appreciation

"Our courteous Lord does not want his servants to despair
because they fall often and grievously; for our failing does not
hinder him in loving us."
—JULIAN OF NORWICH

Often my centering prayer sessions don't
seem to accomplish much. My mind continually bounces around.
I rehearse past hurts and injustices. I think about my task list. I
make plans for the day's meetings. I gain ideas for projects. I have
little sense of the presence of God. I'm distracted.

Yet perhaps these are actually the best days. After all, centering
prayer is not about me and my thoughts. It's about entering a
space outside of my conscious control where I may encounter the
living God. The sessions, when my brain interrupts incessantly,
become opportunities to learn anew about surrender. In these
moments I release whatever captures my attention and return to
a posture of waiting. This may happen dozens of times during
a twenty-minute session. Yet each recitation of my prayer word
serves as an occasion for training in faithfulness and love.

When Jesus was hungry in the wilderness, the tempter pointed
to the presence of an abundant number of stones (Matt. 4:1–4).
He suggested that Jesus use his power to turn them to bread. Jesus
reminded the tempter, "One does not live by bread alone, but by
every word that comes from the mouth of God."

Jesus's hunger was real. He had just completed a forty-day fast. Yet he released it by reciting Scripture as a way of moving away from temptation.

The tempter then presents Jesus with two additional tests (Matt. 4:5–10). As in the first scene, Jesus quotes Scripture and stays focused on God's mission. It is no coincidence that angels appear and attend to Jesus's needs (v. 11). Jesus's self-denial prepared him for God's best rather than the easy way offered by the tempter.

Centering prayer teaches us a similar process of self-denial. Don't mistake self-denial for masochism or mere asceticism. God is not cruel. God is love. The greatest hindrance to our spiritual transformation is ourselves. The process of self-denial prepares us for the deep work that God desires to do in us. Jesus recognized this and modeled a way forward.

Our thoughts are the obstacles that distract us from the work God desires to do in us in solitude. But we must not fight our thoughts. Centering prayer is not about us battling heroically against our distracted minds. Instead, for instance, I calmly use my prayer word, "Jesus," to recenter.

A friend recently asked me if sessions full of distractions frustrated me. The truth of the matter is that they don't any longer. Instead they are the days where I learn the most.

Don't get me wrong. My soul loves the moments of deep contemplation when I become lost in God's love. It is transformational to experience and receive God's unconditional acceptance. It, however, is also transformational to learn anew the lessons taught in silent surrender.

On those days when I'm constantly lost in thought, I learn to focus on appreciation rather than expectation. I remember that centering prayer is not a tactic for engaging God. It is a way of being in which I consciously surrender in love and gratitude to God. I let go of all things that may hinder me, including the expectation that I'll encounter God during my time of prayer.

Releasing thoughts is an act of faith. I trust that God has my best interests at heart. Therefore, my future does not depend on avoiding being lost in a continuous stream of thoughts or even in my ability to recollect the thoughts I released in prayer.

After such sessions, I've learned to appreciate the silence. By releasing the expectation of automatically encountering God in each session, I've found that growth happens. The prayer time is not about me after all. It is not a work that I accomplish. It is resting in the presence of God. Just as the biblical Sabbath envisions life apart from work, centering prayer is an invitation to let go of all human busyness and activity to rest in God.

Lord Jesus Christ, Son of God, have mercy on me, a sinner. Amen.

〇

Now, sit in silence with the Lord. Resist no thought. Retain no thought. React to no thought. Return ever so gently to the sacred word.

CHAPTER 8

Renouncing the Need for the Spectacular

"Even ordinary effort over time yields extraordinary results."
—KEITH ELLIS[44]

I was listening to an interview with a long-time practitioner of centering prayer. She had decades of experience, and as she fielded questions from the audience, someone asked, "Can you share some breakthrough or highlight that you experienced at a weekend prayer retreat?"

I too wanted to hear the practitioner talk about her most memorable encounters with God. However, she refused to answer the question. She reminded the audience that centering prayer is not about chasing deep experiences.

In fact, most of the time in centering prayer is spent discovering how distracted and untidy our minds actually are. For every moment of contemplative connection with the Lord Jesus there are vastly more sessions where we find ourselves repeatedly using our prayer word. In such sessions, we find our inner hamster-wheel brains working on overdrive, lost in thought. Sometimes we will find ourselves so lost in thought that we fail to even use our prayer word to break the pattern. Other times we will sit in silence and fall asleep rather than commune with God.

The key is this: *Commit to making centering prayer a habit and persevere in it.* We are talking about cultivating a practice that flies against the grain of our world. Everything about the twenty-first century screams immediate access and personalized service. With centering prayer, we surrender our need to run the show. It is not a discipline in which our actions drive the activity, such as in reading Scripture, celebrating the Lord's Supper, attending worship services, or serving the poor. These are formative practices, but they are means of grace in which we are active. With centering prayer, we simply sit in silence with our eyes closed and wait upon the Lord. Our "action" consists of showing up and surrendering to the silence. Yet this consistent offering of ourselves in silent prayer to the Lord Jesus will yield a significant harvest over time. But this harvest will likely surprise us. Release any desire for control. Refuse the temptation to think that there is a shortcut.

Know this: *You will encounter the God who loves you.* In the process you will experience not so much what you think you desire, but what you actually need. The places of growth may be unexpected ones. But this is the point. We surrender control by embracing silence before God.

Elijah's flight from Jezebel and encounter with God on Horeb (1 Kings 19) is illustrative. In 1 Kings 18, Elijah had a memorable encounter and public victory over the prophets of Baal. God had literally shown his power and greatness over Baal before the gathered assembly of the people. After defeating the prophets of Baal, Elijah with the help of the people killed all of them. But in the aftermath Queen Jezebel announced that she was going to take vengeance on Elijah and see that he suffered the same fate.

So Elijah fled the land of Israel for Horeb (Mt. Sinai). This was the mountain where God had first called Moses hundreds of years earlier (Exod. 3:1–4:17) and had given God's people the Mosaic Law (Exod. 19:1–Num. 10:10, cf. the book of Deuteronomy).

Elijah went to Horeb to seek the Lord due to the threat against his life and because of his sense of aloneness in his faithfulness.

God provided Elijah a profound lesson. It is a lesson applicable to us as we sit in silence before God. God invited Elijah to stand on Mount Horeb just as Moses had done centuries before. God sent a blistering wind, a great earthquake, and a fire, but Elijah did not encounter God in any of these signs.

God doesn't always or even usually reveal himself in the spectacular. Elijah probably went to Horeb looking for a powerful sign. Instead, Elijah met God in the utter silence (1 Kings 19:12). I'm not suggesting that Elijah was an early practitioner of centering prayer. Instead his story reminds us of how God works. Our flesh may desire a quick fix or an answer on demand. But our soul longs for a real meal that nourishes and replenishes us. Such sustenance comes when we relinquish our demands and wait on the Lord in silence.

Centering prayer involves the intentional surrender of our control. We instead embrace the slow and steady practice of releasing our thoughts in the silence. So don't let early struggles or little evidence of growth discourage you. The practice itself is the point.

Don't keep score and you will likely be astonished over time. During his ministry, Jesus used metaphors of sowing seed, the tiny size of a mustard seed, and the invisible work of yeast to highlight the contrast between the apparent insignificance of small beginnings with the extraordinary gains achieved in time. Søren Kierkegaard wrote, "Life can only be understood backwards; but it must be lived forwards." He was not speaking of centering prayer, but his words capture well my experience. We may not understand or see growth until those times in the future when we turn around to discover that the child of our past has matured.

⌀

Now, sit in silence with the Lord. Resist no thought. Retain no thought. React to no thought. Return ever so gently to the sacred word.

PART TWO

More Biblical/Theological Foundations

CHAPTER 9

Loving the God of Holy Love

"A threefold cord is not quickly broken."

—ECCLESIASTES 4:12B

God can use our time in silent prayer to

cultivate in us higher levels of love for God, neighbor, and self.

The loves of God, neighbor, and self form a cord. In fact, they connect intimately.

God's love serves as the standard for how I am to love my neighbor. Yet simultaneously the way that I love myself also impacts the way that I love others. As we grow in grace, these loves spiral upward together as a thread into a deeper and richer reflection of the One who is Love Divine.

The consistent practice of centering prayer serves as a profound invitation into the deepest levels of God's loving presence and grace. The habits of silence and solitude before God help to integrate the reality of God into the fullness of our human life.

What do I mean by integration? I'm suggesting that many of us have never integrated our rational minds, unconscious minds, deepest emotions (good ones and traumatic ones), and our physical bodies. When we lack this wholeness, we can unconsciously subvert our public commitments and fail to live out the profound truths of our faith.

If asked about the essence of God's character or nature, most will reply, "God is love." But what do we really mean? Is this what we truly believe and feel? Moreover, how do we live in light of the belief that "God is love"? Can we live out God's love consistently?

I've found with a little probing that all is often not what it appears to be. Many of us carry conflicting images and ideas about God that distort our experience of God. Our minds say one thing, but our hearts feel another.

What are some of the common distortions about God that remain unresolved?[45] We often imagine an angry God storming about looking to punish us for our sins. Or we think of God as a kindly grandparent who only smiles at us and holds us to no higher standard. Or we make God equivalent to the impersonal Universe or an Energy that can be accessed through laws or strategies.[46] Or God subtly becomes a projection of our personal values or the values of culture. Or God serves more as an ideology to order life rather than the loving Creator of my soul. All of these images are in reality forms of ancient spiritualities rather than the God whom the Gospel proclaims. Such gods cannot bring us to the depths of love for which our souls long.

In moments of contemplation during meditative prayer, we may find ourselves in deep communion with the God who is love. The deepest moments are often mere glimpses of God's love between waves of our thoughts. Nevertheless, these experiences are powerful. How do we process this reality? How does centering prayer help us to experience and understand God's love and our love for God in more profound ways?

God as Holy Love

In 1 John, the apostle offers two metaphors for God. 1 John 1:5 reads, "God is light and in him there is no darkness at all." 1 John

4 adds, twice: "God is love" (vv. 8 and 16). So according to John, God is light and God is love.

There is a healthy tension between these metaphors. God's light is penetrating and illuminating. As John says in his Gospel concerning the light of Jesus Christ, "The light shines in the darkness, and the darkness did not overcome it" (John 1:5). In other words, light is piercing and pure.

None of us enjoys being seen as we truly are. We prefer to be seen as we *desire* to be seen. We front. We curate an image of ourselves to project a brand to the world. In public we want to be visible on our terms.

We've all seen the opposite of a curated image. Think about political ads where the candidate's opponent is always portrayed with the worst and most sinister-looking photo available. Check out the tabloids at the grocery store and notice the unflattering portraits of celebrities. These images draw us because they play on a deep-seated source of anxiety: *the fear to be known as we truly are.*

In centering prayer there is none of this. We don't have any control over how we appear before God in prayer. But this is the point too, isn't it? When do we ever really have control of our persona before our creator? In centering prayer, we encounter the living God of light who sees, hears, and knows us.

The good news is that God is not a "gotcha god" who is ready to zap us when we miss the mark. In the rest of his letter, John doesn't call God a judge or an accountant or a bookkeeper. Too many of us picture God as an angry judge who is interested in our every mistake and sin. Or God is our mathematics teacher who never gave partial credit. If we missed any part of the problem, it was *all* wrong and we were judged failures. Or God is a raging parent, boss, or spouse who revels in the opportunity to explode over any mistake.

Perhaps in response we've spent decades walking on eggshells with God. We fear that God stands ready to punish and is full of wrath. In an iconic sermon, "Sinners in the Hands of an Angry God" from the Great Awakening in the eighteenth century, Jonathan Edwards preached:

> O sinner! consider the fearful danger you are in: it is a great furnace of wrath, a wide and bottomless pit, full of the fire of wrath, that you are held over in the hand of that God, whose wrath is provoked and incensed as much against you, as against many of the damned in hell. You hang by a slender thread, with the flames of divine wrath flashing about it, and ready every moment to singe it, and burn it apart; and you have no interest in any Mediator, and nothing to lay hold of to save yourself, nothing to keep off the flames of wrath, nothing of your own, nothing that you ever have done, nothing that you can do, to induce God to spare you one moment.[47]

Edwards preached this portrait of God to men, women, and young children. He terrified them into fearful conversions rooted out of a desire to evade eternal damnation.

How much of our personal faith in God finds its origin in a fear of punishment? What is the cost of portraying God this way? Is this what John means by God is light?

Indeed, 1 John says that God is light. God's light brightens, clarifies, and makes visible the reality of who we truly are. It stands as a beacon to life as God intends. God as light is both a lighthouse that guides us but also a searchlight that finds us.

I've worn eyeglasses for most of my life. When you wear glasses, they get dirty. Sometimes you are aware of the fingerprints and dust that collects; other times you are not. If you ever want to see the condition of your glasses, the easiest way is to hold them up to a light. Stunningly, even when you think they are clean, you will see every blemish because the light shows all. God is light. God's light leaves us naked and open to the truth.

When we enter a time of centering prayer, we may well find ourselves in the same sanctuary into which Isaiah once walked. In Isaiah 6:1–8, the prophet found himself in the presence of the holy God. The sight of God was indescribable. The building shook. The smell of incense overpowered. God's heavenly attendants cried out, "Holy, holy, holy is the LORD of hosts; all the earth is full of his glory" (Isa. 6:3). In the presence of the holy one, Isaiah experienced a sense of radical lostness. He lamented, "Woe is me! I am lost, for I am a man of unclean lips, and I live among a people of unclean lips; yet my eyes have seen the King, the LORD of hosts!" (Isa. 6:5). "Woe" is the language of a funeral. In the presence of God, Isaiah felt as though he'd reached the end of his life. He saw dark truths about himself and his people. As far as he could tell, there was no way forward. Yet with God there is always a future. There is suffering and death but there is resurrection and life. At Isaiah's moment of deep need, God cleansed him. Isaiah didn't even request this, but God acted. This is grace.

Isaiah didn't communicate the reason for God's mercy in Isaiah 6, but elsewhere he pointed to God's promises—for example, "though your sins are like scarlet, they shall be like snow; though they are red like crimson, they shall become like wool" (Isa. 1:18).

Why does God forgive sins? Because God is a God of love at the core. This is the witness of the Scriptures. In centering prayer, this can become our experience too.

What It Means for Us that God is Love

God is light and this light can penetrate deep into our being, but God is love. God is light and God is love. Knowing God as love shapes the way we perceive God as light.

Go back to the earliest images of God's response to human brokenness and sin in Genesis 3. Adam and Eve had already eaten the fruit whose consumption God had outlawed. Their eyes had been opened to their nakedness. When they heard God moving toward them in the garden, they hid. Notice God's response carefully and contrast it with the images of a "gotcha god" of popular imagination or a God who separates from us due to our sins.

Instead of hiding, God called out to Adam (Gen. 3:9), "Where are you?"

This is the Good News of the Gospel. Sin creates a fracture in our relationship with God, but it was Adam and Eve who hid from God. God didn't hide from them. Nor does God withdraw from lost people today. He goes looking for them.

When Adam and Eve stepped out from the trees, there were consequences for their actions. But fundamentally God restored their relationship and even extended grace in the form of covering their nakedness (Gen. 3:21). God is looking and calling to each of us today too.

This sort of pattern recurs throughout Scripture. God is light. God's holiness is the antithesis of the darkness of sin and brokenness. It illuminates our lostness. But God's love makes a way forward to a restored relationship and wholeness. These two metaphors stand in balance.

God as the Father Who Loves and Guides Us

The danger of reflecting on God as light is the creation of a wrathful God ready to pounce on any mistake. The danger of God as love is the false portrayal of God as permissive and accepting of all things.

Too often, our culture defines love as *permissive acceptance* of any and all behavior/activity apart from any expectation or standards. God's love is eternal, extends to all people, pursues us in our brokenness, is greater than any human sin, and is the basis for our love of God and for others and ourselves. At the same time, God's light must help shape our understanding of God's love. God is *holy love*. It is a love that is for us. It refuses to leave us where we are. In John's Gospel, Jesus says, "No one has greater love than this, to lay down one's life for one's friends" (John 15:13). Paul echoes this: "But God proves his love for us in that while we still were sinners Christ died for us" (Rom. 5:8).

"See what love the Father has given us, that we should be called children of God; and that is what we are," we read in 1 John 3:1. God as father is a risky image because all of us have a human father. Even the finest fathers wound their children due to their own personal brokenness and need for grace. Those who experienced abuse and/or neglect from their father may recoil from this analogy.

Please hang with me and imagine an ideal father. Good fathers live principled lives that model godly standards and right living. They commit themselves fully to the good of their children and are loyal to their relationships. Their love is unconditional, and they desire for their children to live responsibly. Living responsibly is the essence of faithfulness.

The image of God as father is helpful for holding together the dynamic tension between God as light and God as love. It is a family metaphor. God loves us unconditionally yet shines the light of illumination into even the dark recesses of our souls in order to help us grow and become the persons we were created to be.

How do we live in light of the God who is holy love?

In his modern classic, *New Seeds of Contemplation*, Thomas Merton writes, "Our idea of God tells us more about ourselves than about Him."[48] Through consistent practice of centering prayer, we encounter the living God who loves us and who sent the Son into the world to work for our redemption and who pours out his Spirit on all who believe.

Centering prayer draws us near to the God who has drawn near to us in Jesus Christ. In it we step out of the forest of shame and walk into God's light to experience the God who loves us and died for us.

CHAPTER 10

The Great Commandments and Four Loves

"Love is not a distant point at which we aim with the expectation that one day we will arrive at it and then live happily ever after. Instead, love functions as a goal by directing our day-to-day actions, even the little ones."

—ROBERTA BONDI[49]

The Bible is foundational for our faith and

practice. Contemplative activities such as centering prayer build on our commitments to Scripture. In fact, contemplative practices such as centering prayer can enhance the Spirit's ability to manifest the promises of Scripture in our lives. Our faith then becomes a living and breathing one lived in a moment-by-moment relationship of love for God, love for neighbor, and love for self.

Jesus summarized the teaching of the Torah succinctly in Matthew 22:37–40:

> He said to him, "'You shall love the Lord your God with all your heart, and with all your soul, and with all your mind.' This is the greatest and first commandment. And a second is like it: 'You shall love your neighbor as yourself.' On these two commandments hang all the law and the prophets."[50]

With these words Jesus reaffirmed the Old Testament's authority and summarized its ethic for his followers.

Old Testament Roots of God's Love

From the opening pages of the Bible, we find a different type of God than the gods worshiped by the ancients. The God of the Old and New Testaments is one who desires to bring wholeness, reconciliation, and redemption to a world that desperately needs it.

When Jesus proclaimed the Great Commandment, he was summarizing the teachings of Moses. The Great Commandment is found first in Deuteronomy 6:4–5, and the command to love one's neighbor as oneself is from Leviticus 19:18b.

In Genesis to Deuteronomy critical themes emerge regarding God's love and our response to it.

First, God demonstrates faithfulness by making and keeping promises to Israel's ancestors in Genesis. This begins with the calling of Abraham and Sarah (esp. Gen. 11:27–12:9). We don't have the explicit language of love present, but we find God making unconditional promises of blessing and then faithfully keeping his promises. This is a powerful signal of the reality that God is *with* and *for* God's people for the sake of all people and creation itself (Gen. 1–11).

Second, God reveals his mighty power to save. God does for God's people what they were unable to do for themselves. The core of Israel's gospel is the liberation of God's people from slavery in Egypt (Exod. 1:1–15:21) and the invitation to God's people into a covenantal relationship as God's treasured possession (Exod. 19:3–6).

In the ancient world the gods were always on the side of the well-connected, affluent, and powerful. This was a given. The ancients understood this to be the way that the world works. The religions of Israel's neighbors were about maintenance of the status quo. They were about consolidating and holding onto power by those who already possessed it. Scripture announces a God who breaks into our world and acts on behalf of the oppressed, hurting, and lost. The Exodus was the primary sign of this in the Old Testament. In the New Testament, it is the life, death, and resurrection of Jesus that brings God's story of salvation to a climax. Paul wrote in Romans 5:8, "But God proves his love for us in that while we still were sinners Christ died for us."

Third, in Exodus 34:6–7a, God self-defined his inner character as love. Yes, the Old Testament teaches that God is love. Exodus 34:6–7a reads, "The LORD, the LORD, a God merciful and gracious, slow to anger, and abounding in steadfast love and faithfulness, keeping steadfast love for the thousandth generation, forgiving iniquity and transgression and sin." I refer to this passage as the John 3:16 of the Old Testament. This passage affirms love as the driver of God's actions. It is the reason for God's willingness to forgive and extend grace to God's people and the world. It serves as a counter-testimony to anyone who thinks that the Old Testament presents a God of wrath in contrast to the New Testament's testimony of a God of love. The words in Exodus 34:6–7a reverberate across the Old Testament. They serve as the basis of Moses's prayer for forgiveness of Israel in Numbers 14:13–19. Multiple psalms allude or quote it (see Psalms 77, 103, 145). Jonah cites it to God as the reason he did not want to preach to Nineveh (Jonah 4:2). Jonah feared that God might indeed extend love and mercy to the Ninevites.

Last, the Torah teaches a core ethic of love as the response to God's love. We love because God loved us first. Love is the response of God's people to the love and grace that they received from God. Leviticus 19:18b reads, "Love your neighbor as yourself." Deuteronomy 6:4–5 says, "Hear O Israel, the LORD is our God, the LORD is our one and only.[51] You shall love the LORD your God with all your heart, and with all your soul, and with all your strength." These two commandments serve as the heart of the biblical ethic. The rest of Scripture echoes these commands as the expected response of humanity to God's saving actions and love.

The rest of Scripture reaffirms Moses's core teaching of loving God, neighbor, and self. With the coming of Jesus Christ, we add his saving death and resurrection, followed by the outpouring of the Holy Spirit.

Of course, love is the answer. The Beatles' hit song "All You Need is Love" captured this sentiment for the culture. This obvious value resides at the core of each of us. It is simple to affirm but it is not easy to embody. Even as Scripture lays out love for God and neighbor as core ethical commitments it keenly warns of the obstacles. It will be these very obstacles that a consistent practice of centering prayer will counteract with God's help.

The Danger of Indifference

Before we jump to the New Testament, it is vital to see the human problem that the biblical ethic addresses. If God's design for human relationships involves the love of God and neighbor, what is the opposing view? I ask this question for a practical and spiritual reason. The work God desires to do in us assumes a problem. God calls us to love God, neighbor, and self because most of us become trapped in opposing practices.

We need to take a deep spiritual dive, and this book focuses on the contribution that centering prayer offers to the process of spiritual formation. The contemplative life involves seeing ourselves and God clearly as we actually are, rather than as we wish or hope we are.

So, what is the opposite of love? Most of us quickly respond, "Hate." But this is a mistake. Think about it: *If the choice was love God or hate God and love neighbor or hate neighbor, who would choose hate?*

What is the true opposite of love? Indifference. This is a critical distinction, as it helps us to frame the principal problem we face in our growth in grace. None of us reading this book is going to respond to God's love with hatred. But we may be indifferent to it.

Think about the lessons that one learns from reading Israel's story in the Old Testament, including the narratives of Israel's history (Genesis to Esther) and the message of the prophets (Isaiah to Malachi). God's people struggled to live consistently in a moment-by-moment relationship with the Lord. The Old Testament's honest appraisal remains instructive for us today.

Israel's core problem was its lack of faithfulness to the God who loved God's people and redeemed them from slavery in Egypt. If the opposite of love is indifference, we can truly understand the prophetic critique of God's people. God sent the prophets for two core reasons: *idolatry* and *injustice*.

Idolatry is the main obstacle to our love for God. Israel's problem with the worship and service of other deities was not a lack of belief in the Lord. Israel's problem was its desire to hedge its bets by serving multiple gods and goddesses. This is indifference at its core. Love for God according to the Great Commandment (Deut. 6:4–5) assumes an undivided commitment to God as our "one and only." Think of it this way: It is difficult to love and serve the one true God when our hearts and minds are caught up with many little gods.

Growth in grace involves moving toward a whole-person response of love for God. Centering prayer helps us recognize where in our lives our hearts are divided—where we say we love God with our lips, but our feet and hands suggest otherwise.

Injustice is indifference to the command to love one's neighbor. Israel's problem wasn't that God's people hated others. Hatred involves outright hostility and intentionality. Israel's problem involved its definition of neighbor. This led for example to the abuse of the poor by neglecting to hold all to the high standard of equality under God's law. If we define neighbor narrowly enough, we easily create excuses for selfishness and injustice.

Clearly, indifference is not merely an Old Testament problem. For example, in Ephesians 5, Paul gives a rousing exhortation to wise and holy living. This involves embracing the light and fleeing the darkness. There is no middle path, so he writes, "Sleeper, awake! Rise from the dead, and Christ will shine on you" (Eph. 5:14). More well-known is the warning to the church of Laodicea in the book of Revelation: "I know your works; you are neither cold nor hot. I wish that you were either cold or hot. So, because you are lukewarm, and neither cold nor hot, I am about to spit you out of my mouth" (Rev. 3:15–16).

Idolatry and injustice are problems because they diminish people and thwart God's mission to love others. Out of a love for God flows love for neighbor and love for self. In response to the grace and love of God, we move toward others in loving mission. As my friend Alex McManus frames it, "The Gospel comes to us on its way to someone else." God pours his love into our hearts so that it can overflow to others. Indifference has no place in love and mutes its power.

In Romans 13:8–10 Paul profoundly demonstrates how the commandment to love others is the fulfillment of the entire

Mosaic law. Romans 13:8 points to a critical element: "Owe no one anything, except to love one another; for the one who loves another has fulfilled the law." Paul emphasizes that love is active. *Of course it is*, we respond. But the issue runs deeper. It is easier to not do something (a negative standard), and this creates a false sense of accomplishment. Paul goes on in verse nine to quote from the Ten Commandments. He lists the commands against adultery, murder, theft, and coveting. Coveting is an internal sin of idolatry/greed. If one does not take action on it, it is an unseen sin. Of the others, should we applaud ourselves daily for our advanced spiritual life because we managed not to kill anyone, not to commit adultery, or to refrain from stealing? I would call this type of life a neutral one rather than a robust life of love.

How many of us feel guilty by our desires (that which we covet) and content ourselves with sin avoidance or the suppression of our desires? For how many of us does this represent the best Christian life? Yet this is merely the minimum standard.

Look at Romans 13:8 again: "Owe no one anything, except to love one another; for the one who loves another has fulfilled the law." This is a *maximal* standard. This debt is ongoing. It involves engaging others positively rather than the mere avoidance of negative actions toward others. It points to the ongoing need to grow in love as a means of loving God and others. Observe the source of our love for others. We love because God first loves us.

Love Your Neighbor as Yourself

When I think about God's will, I generally describe it in a shorthand as love for God and love for neighbor. But this leaves a key love out of the equation. The second command is not "Love your neighbor." It is "Love your neighbor *as yourself.*" The Bible assumes self-love. What does it mean to love ourselves? Why is this critical for loving our neighbor? How does this circle back to a love for God as the greatest of the commandments?

At stake is the issue of reciprocity. I love my neighbor as I love myself. This reminds us of several other statements by Jesus.

"Do unto others as you'd have them do unto you," and "Forgive us our debts as we forgive our debtors." We may also add the so-called "Silver rule" found in the early Christian writing *Didache* as a further clarification of loving one's neighbor as oneself: "And whatsoever thou wouldst not have done to thyself, do not thou to another" (I.2).[52]

I fully recognize that we are treading on slippery ground. To talk about self-love may sound profoundly selfish and self-absorbed. It can be. It may cause us to feel uncomfortably close to New Age spirituality. It may remind some of the excesses of the "self-esteem" movement. It may strike others as a theologically problematic term drawn from our psycho-therapeutic culture. I will take the risk, for I believe that to truly love God and neighbor with all that we are involves learning to love ourselves.[53]

St. Bernard's Four Levels of Love

To take it a step further, what if the highest form of loving God is loving yourself?

To answer this question, allow me to introduce the medieval reformer Bernard of Clairvaux (c. 1090–1153). Bernard produced a profound work, *On Loving God*. In this treatise, he sketches out the soul's journey from self-centered love to a self-love centered on God.[54]

The lowest level is simply loving oneself for the sake of oneself. This is a self-love rooted in self-interest and personal gain. I sense that you, as a reader of this book, have long left this level or at least have the self-awareness to move forward in your growth in grace.

The second level of love is the point at which we engage the Divine. The self begins a relationship with God, but it is a love for God for the sake of oneself. This is religion at its lowest level. We seek God for what God can do for us. Our relationship is purely transactional. God serves as a cosmic giver of gifts and the miraculous rescuer (*deus ex machina*) who delivers us in times of trouble. This is a level of spiritual formation that is interested in maintaining the status quo if life is good and petitioning for help when life disappoints.

At the third level, we begin to enter the deeper realms of spirituality. As we grow in grace, God works in us, and we begin to love God for God's sake. In other words, we love God for who God truly is and what God has done. Our spiritual journey becomes God-focused. We are no longer selfishly fixed on personal needs, wants, and desires. God's beauty and love captivate us. Our focus is on self-denial and a conscious surrender to the God of grace. We may sense that we are "all in" for God and God's mission. We give of ourselves. We consciously practice our Christianity. Some of us may even enter into religious vocations. This is the level of grace that tends to be modeled for us as the highest form of devotion. For years, I believed that this represented my full devotion to the Lord. I can remember my pastor during my formative years talking about "dying daily to self." But friends, I want you to know that God has more for us than loving God for God's sake.

Rooted in the Shema

Some may be wondering what is more profound than loving God for God's sake. Bernard believed there was a higher supreme love. It is a return to self-love, but a self-love that has nothing to do with selfishness. Bernard describes in this way: "Self-interest is restrained within due bounds when love supervenes; for then it rejects evil things altogether, prefers better things to those merely good, and cares for the good only on account of the better. In like manner, by God's grace, it will come about that man will love his body and all things pertaining to his body, for the sake of his soul. He will love his soul for God's sake; and he will love God for Himself alone."[55]

In a similar fashion, Irenaeus, the second-century Church Father, in *Against Heresies* wrote, "The glory of God is man fully alive."

Thomas Merton captures this vision well: "Occupy my whole life with the one thought and the one desire of love, that I may love not for the sake of merit, not for the sake of perfection, not for the sake of virtue, not for the sake of sanctity, but for you alone."[56]

Centering prayer helps. We'll explore this in the remainder of the book.

CHAPTER 11

The Fear of God as the Freedom for Love

"There is no fear in love, but perfect love casts out fear;
for fear has to do with punishment, and whoever fears
has not reached perfection in love."

—1 JOHN 4:18

What about the "fear of God"? We just explored God as love, but the "fear of the Lord" is a persistent theme in Scripture too. It remains a driver in our inner world. Many of us live our lives in response to fears. These may be conscious or unconscious, but they likely control us more than we may realize.

For many the command to "Fear God" is a counter-narrative that challenges the portrait of love that we sketched out in the previous chapters. Some of us may struggle starting a centering prayer practice out of a fear of God. The thought of sitting with God may sound like a scary proposition.

This chapter offers a way to think about why the Bible says, "Fear God," while simultaneously affirming God's love and our need to live out love for God, neighbor, and self. The pathway for resolving this tension involves the reality that whatever we fear likely exerts control over us and constricts our ability to love fully.

When we read the Old Testament, we find texts such as, "The fear of the LORD is the beginning of knowledge; fools despise wisdom and instruction" (Prov. 1:7). In Deuteronomy 10:12, there is a cluster of phrases associated with practicing a faithful walk with the Lord. Observe how this verse begins, "So now, O Israel, what does the LORD your God require of you? *Only to fear the LORD your God*, to walk in all his ways, to love him, to serve the LORD your God with all your heart and with all your soul" (Deut. 10:12, my emphasis).

God's love does not negate our need for fear. In fact, Scripture's call to "Fear God" serves as a check against any attempt to understand God's love as a permissive love apart from holiness. We saw this in our discussion of the images of God as light and God as love from 1 John in chapter nine. Yet, questions persist. What kind of a God demands and expects fear from would-be worshipers? Will I be frightened by the presence of God during a centering prayer session?

Is Fear of God a Thing of the Past?

We often seek to redefine fear in terms of "reverence" or "awe." These definitions are helpful, but "reverence" and "awe" risk missing a key takeaway.

What do we mean by "reverence" and "awe"? Let's ponder this. We may feel a sense of reverence and awe in the presence of something bigger than we are. For example, I've felt reverence and awe standing on the edge of the Grand Canyon. I felt small. This type of awe and reverence is clearly present in terms of God, but there is more. We don't experience reverence and awe for God merely because of his infinite or transcendent nature. It is not a matter of feeling like a gnat in the presence of an elephant.

A biblical response of reverence and awe comes through an encounter with God's holy love. God is undivided in terms of motivation, actions, and character. God models holiness. Part of our fear is a natural response to God's moral perfection and our lack. In the presence of God's holiness, we may feel unworthy of God's love and often ashamed and guilty. So there are two aspects to the fear of God. One is our response to God's awesomeness and otherness. The other is due to our lack of holy character.

Should we try to recapture a genuine fear of God? Is this a relic from a superstitious past that we as spiritually evolved moderns need to move away from? I'm not ready to give up on fear just yet. As I wrestle with Scripture, I believe that fear is a component needed in our relationship with God.

Let's face it. We are all afraid of something. Most of us are afraid of many things. Psychology teaches us that fear drives us. We fear death. We fear being alone. We fear being bad parents. We fear not having enough money. We fear being found out. We fear letting others down. We fear that we are not enough. These fears limit us and shackle us from becoming the people God created us to be. In fact, our fears are a form of idolatry. That which we fear becomes a god to us.

I remember waking up one night many years ago hearing my Great Dane Sir Morpheus Maximus growling. It was in November a week or so after Halloween. Morpheus was upset. When I opened my bedroom door, I could smell his fear. Dogs release a pungent scent when frightened. He was at the opposite end of the house. His hair was standing on end. He was terrified. As I cautiously moved forward to assess the situation, I caught sight of the object of Morpheus's horror. I suddenly shifted from concern to laughter. A Mylar balloon in the shape of a ghost had lost the last of its helium during the night and had lowered from its ceiling perch to the floor. In a heartbeat, the balloon ghost had transformed my 160-pound dog into Scooby Doo. I put the balloon in a spare bedroom and headed back to bed. As I pulled up the covers, I reflected on Morpheus's ordeal. I smiled and thought, *We are all afraid of something, aren't we?*

This is where the importance of Scripture's call to fear the Lord comes in. The Bible is a powerful book precisely in its ability to describe the human heart and condition. It reflects on our ambitions and dreams. It recognizes our potential for both greatness and failure. It does not sugarcoat life. It knows our motivations. It calls out self-centered ambitions. It challenges us to realign ourselves with the ethic and purposes of God's kingdom. To do this, it provides new frameworks for understanding our inner drives. The fear of the Lord is one of these frameworks.

Modern psychology summarizes our drives into two categories: avoidance of pain and the pursuit of pleasure. To put it another way, our two primary motivators are fear and love. Fear plays a crucial role in helping us to avoid pain and harm. Fear keeps us alive in moments when we face life-threatening scenarios. But the problem lies in the objects of our fear. If we fear the wrong things, we may miss out on God's larger vision for our lives.

In fact, fear can lead to subtle forms of idolatry. Whatever we fear controls us. If our internal fear response served us in the past to warn us of danger, this fear can begin to gain power over us. This can thwart the work of God in our lives.

Sitting before God in silence in centering prayer will often reveal past pain points that often find their root in fear. Let me share a memory that first churned up in a centering prayer session.

When I was in fourth grade, I had a teacher who controlled our class by raising her voice to threatening levels. I vividly remember returning to school after being absent due to an illness. As soon as the opening bell rang, my teacher announced that she needed to have a heart-to-heart talk with the class. This caused me to lower my guard because in my family the language of "heart to heart" always led to deep but affirming conversations wrapped in love.

But I soon discovered that to my teacher "heart to heart" meant publicly dressing down the class. To this day I've never heard my parents raise their voices in anger at one another or at me. So as a nine-year-old fourth grader, I found the teacher's angry tone was terrifying. Then, she called me to stand up in front of the class, stuck a paper in my face, and screamed, "Brian! Is this yours?" I was shaking and couldn't think straight. She yelled it again. I took the paper and there was no name on it. She told me that it was subpar work and that I should be ashamed of myself for its poor quality as well as for not writing my name at the top. Tears flowed from my eyes. I was a sensitive child. This added to my shame and embarrassment as I felt the eyes of the whole class on me. I meekly said, "I'm sorry. I always do my best." To this, she replied, "Your best is not good enough today. Get back to your seat."

She moved on to another student, and I had a chance to collect myself. As I looked at the paper, I realized that it was not mine. I had not even been in school the day that the class turned in this particular assignment. Yet I was too scared to speak up. I never even told my parents what happened.

This event left scars that have followed me into adulthood. The sound of an adult screaming in anger triggers me and turns me back into a terrified little boy. Over the years, I've withheld my opinions and not spoken truth out of the fear that another might yell at me. This fear became a chain that bound me. It's caused me harm in relationships. It's given certain personality types more power over me than I'd care to admit. It's caused me to act cowardly at times when I had an opportunity to step into a situation and act for good. Fear has robbed me of much potential joy.

Through centering prayer, I've been able to release this painful memory and recognize my hurt. I still don't care to hear adults raising their voices, but I'm slowly recognizing that my response is one rooted in my childhood and that I'm no longer a nine-year-old boy being screamed at by an out-of-control teacher. I am able to take action now during heated conflict rather than cowering as I did that day in class.

It is vital then for us to face our fears. Ask yourself: What do I fear? What truly troubles me? What do I most seek to avoid? What triggers me?

Our answers provide guidance to the chains that bind us. For we become slaves and prisoners of our fears. No matter how many times a speaker or author exhorts us to move past fear, it is simply not that easy. Fear is part of the human experience. It sits deep within us.

This brings us back to Scripture and its consistent exhortation to "Fear the LORD." This is not merely an Old Testament idea that the New Testament replaces with love. The New Testament also contains positive statements about the fear of God. Consider a few texts:

Acts 9:31: "Meanwhile the church throughout Judea, Galilee, and Samaria had peace and was built up. Living in the fear of the Lord and in the comfort of the Holy Spirit, it increased in numbers."

Philippians 2:12b: "Work out your own salvation with fear and trembling."

1 Peter 2:17: "Honor everyone. Love the family of believers. Fear God. Honor the emperor."

God wants to be our "one and only" (Deut. 6:4). The God of the Bible is not merely one among many. God is not simply an energy field that permeates the universe. God is our creator who figuratively sits on high. As the psalmist declares, "Who is like the LORD our God, who is seated on high, who looks far down on the heavens and the earth?" (Ps. 113:5–6).

The need for the fear of the Lord finds its roots in human nature. We are programmed for fear. Fear protects us from harm. It is not a matter of eliminating our fears but rather aligning fear with its only legitimate object. To fear any part of creation is to dishonor the Creator. It is God who gives life. It is God who created the very things that we fear. It is God alone who will ultimately render judgment on our lives. Thus, to fear anything or anyone other than our Creator is to practice a form of idolatry.

The irony is, if I want to live freely without fear, I must only fear the LORD. This is not because God is scary or vindictive or cruel or unhinged. It is because only God deserves our fear. This statement does not necessarily go down easily, but it is vital medicine for us as we seek to live and grow into the people whom God created us to be.

As we saw in the previous chapter, Scripture speaks against two grave dangers to faith and life: idolatry and injustice. When we lose our fear for God, we open ourselves up to these negatives.

The only Being that Scripture commands us to fear *loves us unconditionally*. When the only object of our fear is the God who loves us, we are free. Free from cruel taskmasters. Free from the manipulation of ideology. Free from the cultural pressures that suffocate and promote a false conformity.

Instead, we are free to love God, free to love others, and free to love ourselves. In deep moments of contemplation in centering prayer, I've experienced true "oneness" with God's loving "is-ness."

In these moments, I've experienced the perfect love that casts out all fear that Scripture describes. Profoundly in such moments, fear of God morphs into a deeper way to love God rooted in freedom from all false objects of fear.

PART THREE

Thinking About
Our Thoughts

CHAPTER 12

Hamster-Wheel Minds

"Can we be free to let go of what's unimportant? In dying to
the things that frighten and bind us most, can we embrace a
fearlessness that frees us to love fiercely?"
—BELDEN LANE[57]

As we sit in silence before God, it is our
work to release our thoughts and recenter using the sacred word.
But this act is more about a surrender into rest than a task. The
challenge is learning to recognize our thoughts and then trusting
God enough to return to our silent meditative prayer regardless
of how interesting, emotionally charged, helpful, or troubling a
thought itself may be.

Five Common Thoughts

Keating describes five types of thoughts that pray-ers will
encounter.[58]

"The woolgathering of the imagination."

These thoughts are the typical sensory data that run nonstop in
our minds. These encompass the multitude of thoughts, images,
feelings, and emotions that flow through our minds continuously.
They also include sounds and stimuli that we sense during our
prayer time. As we enter solitude with God, we may begin to float
above this flow and abide in God's presence.

"Thoughts with an emotional attraction to them."

These may be good or bad thoughts that invite our attention and reflection. They can be insights into questions we've been pondering. They may be pleasant memories or ideas or even goals worth pursuing.

We will find ourselves lured into our thought stream by memories, images, ideas, feelings, or even noises (birds chirping, a car starting, etc.). When this occurs and we become aware of it, we use our prayer word to return to the Lord.

In addition to memories, we may find ourselves in possession of a good idea. We may suddenly gain access to an insight that solves a problem at home or work. Perhaps we remember something to say, or we suddenly recall a task undone. The temptation is to try to hold onto the idea lest we forget it. Perhaps we even put our prayer time on hold and reach for a notebook to record it. Yet to do so would work against our intention to be with God.

This is an opportunity to exercise deep trust. Ask yourself: Do I trust that God has my best interests at heart? If the answer is "yes," then simply surrender your need to try to remember or record the thought by returning to God with your prayer word. Trust God to bring the idea back to mind later in the day if it truly is one worth remembering at all.

M. Basil Pennington, who cofounded the modern centering prayer revival with Thomas Keating, presents a helpful analogy regarding the type of interruption that occurs.[59] He likens using our prayer word to entering a pool and swimming underwater. Typically, before diving in, we prepare ourselves by taking a number of deep breaths in ritual fashion. Likewise, at the beginning of centering prayer, we often prepare our hearts with a few moments in which we set our intention.

As I shared in chapter two, I use the Jesus prayer at the beginning of my time in silence: "Lord Jesus Christ, Son of God, have mercy on me, a sinner." Implicit in this preparation is my intention to be present with the Lord. This means an upfront surrender of thoughts, agendas, and time to God.

Upon the plunge into the pool, I will eventually find that I need to return to the surface for a breath. But unlike the case of my initial plunge, I do not have to engage in the ritual of preparing to swim; I simply take a breath and slip back under the surface. In centering prayer, this is the gentle exercise of the prayer word.

"Insights, and psychological breakthroughs."

Times of solitude often create moments of inspiration for us. A deep insight into our spiritual formation may come into our awareness. New personal breakthroughs are a tempting distraction. The false self fears missing out. Yet we must practice self-denial and realign with the intention to be with God in prayer. To turn away from a new insight takes deep faith.[60]

I find this category of thought challenging. Pennington describes it as the temptation to monitor or remember the thoughts, ideas, images, and feelings that we experience during the time of prayer.[61] Early on in centering prayer, I used to reflect on my time in my journal. I'd write whether I judged the session good or bad. I even attempted to capture in writing any thoughts or emotions that I encountered while in prayer. Such a practice, I now realize, subtly defeats our intention to surrender because *we* remain in control. Our stated desire is to be *present* fully with God, yet some part of us attempts to be attentive to preserving the experience rather than being in the *now*.

This category of distracting thought remains an ongoing temptation for me because I like to optimize my life. I'm always looking for hacks, tactics, and technologies that allow me to increase my efficiency and productivity. Thus, my tendency at the beginning of my centering prayer journey was to evaluate each session in order to figure out a system that maximized the time with God. I did this in two ways. First, I evaluated body position, atmosphere, and time of day. Second, I journaled both the good and difficult thoughts, emotions, images, and ideas that came to mind. In other words, instead of simply releasing these thoughts, I tried simultaneously to release them yet still *remember* them. This is the heart of the monitor. I wanted the memories in my journal as a means of assessing my own growth. Insidiously, this put me rather than God in control. I told myself that I was doing this in order to grow spiritually with God, but I was really blocking the work God desired to do in me.

The compulsion to create a system for spiritual growth may be in fact an enemy of deep communion with God. Pennington writes:

> The whole evaluating system of our culture and society supports it. We are very production-oriented. To do something and not keep track of what is coming out of it is very alien to our usual way of functioning, even in prayer. We find our value and affirm the worth of ourselves, our activities, and our very existence, according to our productivity. To let go and forget about producing and just be and enjoy is a natural gift we have virtually lost.[62]

We become addicted to the monitor because it feeds our false self. The false self desires control of our life. This desire to control is the root of sin. Remember God's words to Cain before Abel's murder: "Sin is lurking at the door; its desire is for you, but you must master it" (Gen. 4:7b). The antidote to moving through monitoring thoughts is not trying harder, but dying. Paul wrote in 1 Corinthians 15:31, "I die every day!" The false self dies when we starve it of the attention and control that it desires. The means to this end is *surrender*. We cannot outthink, out-scheme, or out-work the false self. It slowly dies by our returning gently to the Lord in prayer over and over, moment by moment. As Pennington says, "Centering Prayer is very simple, but it is not easy, precisely because it does involve the death to self—the false, fabricated self—in order to be able to be and to live wholly unto God. Nobody wants to die."[63]

"Self-reflection"

Some of our thoughts focus on what is occurring in the silence. They flow into the mind in response to deep communion. We may become aware of the depth of the peace we are experiencing during our prayer time. This awareness then becomes a distraction. The only way forward is to turn again to the sacred word in conscious surrender.

You find yourself in this thought whenever you think, *Wow. I've surrendered all of my thoughts.* Or, *I'm enjoying sitting in silent communion with God.* Notice the irony. The actual recognition of the depth of our experience in centering prayer becomes a distraction that pulls us away from communion with God. As with all thoughts, our response is to gently recenter with our prayer word.

"Interior Purification"

The deepest work of centering prayer turns on our response to thoughts related to "interior purification." Such thoughts are the parts of the unconscious that emerge from the depths of deep peace. Keating refers to this dynamic as "a kind of divine psychotherapy."[64] God's love works to cleanse and free us from the false and shadow self. God brings light into the dark crevices of our inner being. Practitioners may be confronted with their true motivations for certain actions and see portraits of themselves that are far removed from their public persona. This is the beginning of the healing of the false self with its shadow and the reappearance of our true self.

Again, our response involves refusing to dwell on the thoughts, emotions, and memories. We gently release them by reciting our prayer word.

The category of interior purification involves thoughts that create tension in our lives. These are the demons that we face when we journey within. The temptation is to begin to judge ourselves and focus on the content of the thought. This will often create more inner turmoil as we attempt to deal with the pain out of our own resources. We may feel guilt, shame, anger, or lack due to what comes into the mind's eye. We may suddenly experience thoughts such as *I'm not enough* or *I don't do enough* or *I don't have enough*. They can easily pull us all the way back to the surface in our prayers. Yet the antidote again is the gift of surrender. We return gently to the Lord.

This process of letting go of pain rather than suppressing it or focusing on it is one of the ways that God's grace brings healing to our lives through centering prayer. We move forward by dying to our need to control and trusting that God's grace is a true healing balm.

The Grace of Apatheia

Of all the thoughts that we learn to surrender, the most troubling are the ones that occur when our unconscious unloads.

We will encounter the truth of our inner world. Past hurts, grudges, pain, regrets, sinful patterns, and wounds will emerge.

I often warn beginning students of centering prayer to be ready to face their inner demons.[65] During sessions, I've encountered the best and worst of my life played back in cinematic fashion. This is part of the healing process of centering prayer. We must be prepared for what bubbles to the surface. We must not suppress these thoughts. Your initial inclination will likely be to pull back in fear, guilt, and shame.

There is a dramatic scene in *Lord of the Rings: The Return of the King*. It occurs during the siege of Minas Tirith. The forces of evil threaten to overrun this last bastion of the kingdom of Gondor. The wizard Gandalf attempts to bolster the morale and defenses at the main city gate. He knows the terrifying strength of the forces of darkness including orcs and trolls that the human defenders will soon face. As a flaming battering ram breeches the gate, Gandalf proclaims, "You are soldiers of Gondor, no matter what comes through that gate you will stand your ground." He is calling for calmness and courage in the face of fear.

Such a courageous serenity is the spirit with which we need to face painful thoughts and memories so that we can *surrender* them by using our prayer word. Through the process of nonresistance to and surrender of troubling thoughts, God will gradually facilitate our inner purification. The ancients had a word for this attitude or trait of nonresistance: *apatheia*.[66] Our modern words "apathy" and "apathetic" find their roots in this ancient idea, but our modern words are misleading. Apatheia is not a state of non-emotion or uncaring. Rather it is the avoidance of excessive emotion. This means gaining an awareness of how certain thoughts or circumstances trigger strong inner judgments that create powerful emotional responses.

Apatheia keeps us from reacting to our pain and to our sins in ways that magnify the intensity of the emotion. It serves as a hedge against judging ourselves harshly. Our temptation when confronted by a difficult thought is to make the recognition of the painful emotion mean something more than it does.

Instead of battling the thought that creates a disordered emotion, we learn to respond nonreactively. Perhaps a sign of nonreactivity may in some cases be joy and peace that God has revealed to us something. It is even possible to learn to be grateful in the midst of confronting our untamed emotions. God after all is with us in the process.

Thus, apatheia "is shown in an ability to face things, memories and dreams without being ruffled."[67] This is critical in centering prayer. It is not a freedom from emotion. It is a freedom from untamed emotions (conscious or unconscious) that may drive behavior contrary to the love of God, neighbor, and self.

Centering prayer cultivates apatheia through the surrender of our attachment to our thoughts—even those held deep within us. Learning to surrender frees us from stressful thoughts that require purification and for the possibility of focusing love on what matters most: for God, neighbor, and oneself.[68] The cultivation of apatheia allows one to separate harmful desires from ones that truly serve our growth into the person God created us to be.[69] As we grow, our ability to respond to our thoughts—no matter how beautiful or how troubling—out of a state of apatheia increases.

Whether a thought is beautiful or disturbing, we learn to receive it, notice it, and surrender it. This is apatheia at work. Apatheia is a good description of the inner state of mind that we slowly cultivate as we sit in silence in anticipation of communion with God.

CHAPTER 13

Inner Purification and Growth in Love

"Hence monastic prayer, especially meditation and contemplative prayer, is not so much a way to find God as a way of resting in him whom we have found, who loves us, who is near to us, who comes to draw us to himself."

—THOMAS MERTON[70]

The release rather than the suppression

of painful and sometimes embarrassing thoughts is where I've experienced the greatest healing in my life. Centering prayer has been catalytic in my growth.

I remember early in my centering prayer practice that I found myself lost in a sexual thought. When I realized that I was in a thought loop, I felt tremendous shame. There I was sitting in silence with the intention of spending time with God and instead I found myself thinking about sex. I thought something was wrong with me. How could I be having this sort of thought in the context of prayer? Little did I realize, at the time, but this is common. Moreover, it was part of the process of healing for me.

In fact, the recognition of troubling thoughts goes back to the beginning of the monastic movement. The fourth-century desert father Evagrius Ponticus wrote about "distracting thoughts." He is one of the key figures who laid roots for what is now known as centering prayer.

Evagrius's Eight Distracting Thoughts

Evagrius isolated eight categories of distracting thoughts that may come to mind when sitting in silence.[71] He was a monk who withdrew from society to embrace an ascetic life of solitude in the desert. Here are two passages in which he reflects on the experience of praying in silence and solitude. His words offer a warning about the presence of painful and troubling thoughts:

> When the devils see that you are really fervent in your prayer they suggest certain matters to your mind, giving you the impression that there are pressing concerns demanding attention. In a little while they stir up your memory of these matters and move your mind to search into them. Then when it meets with failure it becomes saddened and loses heart.

> The devil so passionately envies the man who prays that he employs every device to frustrate that purpose. Thus he does not cease to stir up thoughts of various affairs by means of the memory. He stirs up all the passions by means of the flesh. In this way he hopes to offer some obstacle to that excellent course pursued in prayer on the journey to God.[72]

Evagrius's eight categories are gluttony, impurity (or lust), avarice, sadness, anger, spiritual sloth, vanity, and pride. He recognized that we are powerless to control when these thoughts arise. He attributed them to the devil. He insisted, however, that it is in our power to surrender these thoughts to God rather than to dwell on them.[73]

Don't stumble over the "devil" language, here. Whether or not you share Evagrius's belief that these thoughts are directed by evil spirits or whether you prefer to read his language symbolically for what emerges out of the swamplands of our inner being, Evagrius describes well the terrain that we encounter in our journey to God in centering prayer.

In Evagrius's time, Christianity had become the recognized religion of the Roman Empire. With the protection of the state there was very little personal risk for people to identify with the Christ-following movement. In fact, the Church began to consolidate its power and, in some locales, even persecuted those who practiced the former religions of the empire.

The men and women who entered the desert did so to find a purer form of the faith. The desert fathers were zealous for the ways of God and renounced the wider world. Yet they discovered a profound lesson that remains true for us. In their times of prayer, they struggled with the very thoughts and passions that they presumed they'd left behind in the world.

Centering prayer is transformative because we come face to face with our inner demons. They emerge in the practice of silence. But God will be present when they come, and we can find transformation by surrendering them to our loving Lord with our prayer word. All we have to muster is the courage to be still. This is the state of apatheia that we explored in the previous chapter. Evagrius considered the state of apatheia to be the proper state for prayer.[74]

When we read early Christian theologians, we find all of these categories described as the "passions."[75] We can think of these as emotionally driven drives or compulsions. We may understand all of Evagrius's categories as disordered or excessive expressions of emotions.

These emotions are disordered primarily because they are a form of idolatry. They compete with the core command of loving God with all that we are. When allowed to drive our actions, these disordered emotions elevate aspects of life to a position where they compete with our love for God alone as our one and only. The work of surrender de-elevates these false gods to their proper place under the lordship of Jesus. When we surrender our disordered emotions, we are increasing our capacity to love God unfettered by the swamplands within.

The practice of centering prayer does its work of inner purification by allowing our disordered affections to rise to our mind's eye. We surrender the thought by returning to our prayer word. Over time, we build muscle memory and do this more and more easily.

I was shocked by what unloaded out of my unconscious over time. No one had warned me about this.

Gluttony

Gluttony is about privileging the physical condition of the body over love for God. At its core, it is about an excessive obsession with food. It's the idea that, if only I ate this or that, I'd experience wholeness and satisfaction. Gluttony is not merely about overeating. It is also about excessive concern for food. Sometimes, our modern focus on health foods, superfoods, biohacking, and body-sculpting can arise from a gluttonous spirit. The intention here is not to condemn healthy practices but to recognize that such practices may hinder our spiritual development when they become disordered. Evagrius specifically faced monks whose excessive focus on illness or hunger tempted them to give up their spiritual practices.

Jesus's teaching from the Sermon on the Mount comes to mind. Consider Matthew 6:25, "Therefore I tell you, do not worry about

your life, what you will eat or what you will drink, or about
your body, what you will wear. Is not life more important than
food . . .?" Jesus concludes this with a critical principle for life:
"But strive first for the kingdom of God and his righteousness,
and all these things will be given to you as well" (6:33). His
words serve as a reminder that food has its place but not in the
throne room of our hearts.

During centering prayer, images of food may arise, or
one may also experience feelings of inadequacy about one's
body type. This may include fantasies about one's ideal body.
Observe these sensations and thoughts and then gently return
to the silence by using your prayer word.

Impurity/Lust

The second of the distracting thoughts involves a hot
button issue in our day: disordered sexuality or impurity.
Impurity involves lust and fornication. It is the objectification
or depersonalization of another soul in the service of our
desires. Like the need for physical food, the human libido is a
powerful drive. God created human sexuality as a good gift, but
its disordered expression can wreak havoc. Evagrius's writings
are explicit in how sexual thoughts and fantasy can challenge
even the most devout monk's devotion to Jesus as Lord.

Our present world is an odd mix of hypersexualized and
repressive cultures sometimes living in proximity to one
another. The church bears many scars of disordered sexuality.

I've found many Christian brothers and sisters who repressed
their sexual drives due to negative lessons learned from strict
parents or in the teachings of the church. The message is
mixed but often sounds like this: sex is a gift from God; it is
for pleasure and procreation, but it can only be expressed in

a marriage between a man and a woman. Any other expression is sinful.

This often makes the topic taboo. Yet as experience shows, one does not have the privilege of turning on and off sexual thoughts and desires until one is married, and married persons still may struggle with their sexual drives and desires. We can understand the theology of the body and the beauty of sexual love in our minds, but our unconscious drives do not always line up with our theological convictions. [76] This is true for married, single, and divorced heterosexuals, let alone for persons in the LGBTQ+ community.

In my own life as well as through years of mentoring others, I've experienced and listened to struggles stemming from a repressed sexual shadow. The church has done an excellent job of warning about disordered sexuality, but it has not always offered a positive vision for a healthy one that recognizes the sexual nature of human life while providing resources and instructions for the proper ordering of the erotic apart from the suppression of its disordered expressions.

In fact, sexual energy fuels the clandestine struggles of our time with promiscuity, affairs, dissatisfaction in marriage, the oppression of women, pornography, and sexual harassment. There have been too many public reports of sexual brokenness among church leaders to miss the signals. From the recent scandals within Roman Catholicism to the fall of prominent megachurch pastors accused of inappropriate conduct, there is sufficient smoke in the air to signal a fire is burning.

Centering prayer helps us to confront and acknowledge repressed parts of our sexual nature. Speaking of this, Ó Madagáin writes,

When sexual repression has taken place, people often have difficulty in relating to others in an intimate or truly caring way. This can be a serious impediment to our work or ministry and in a marriage relationship. Since sexual energy is so powerful, it is very important that it is properly integrated or it may emerge in mid-life with twice as much force as it did in adolescence, with obviously dangerous consequences.[77]

In silence, sexual fantasies and thoughts may arise. No matter how alluring or troubling they may be, surrender them to God and return to the silence.

Avarice/Greed

The third distracting thought is avarice. Avarice is often thought of as greed. But to limit avarice to greed misses its subtleties. Avarice is a disordered desire for wealth. Jesus warns about the allure of wealth throughout the Gospels. In the Sermon on the Mount, he said,

> Do not store up for yourselves treasures on earth, where moth and rust consume and where thieves break in and steal; but store up for yourselves treasures in heaven, where neither moth nor rust consumes and where thieves do not break in and steal. For where your treasure is there your heart will be also. (Matt. 6:19–21)

Avarice is a distraction to both the rich and the poor. Avarice is the enthronement in our hearts of the illusion that wealth creates ultimate security. It is not merely conspicuous consumption. It can also be the expectation that others will provide for you. A sense of entitlement for charity because of one's religious vows of poverty is just as much a sign of avarice as a sports star's obsession with owning luxury cars. It can even be the obsessive focus on saving for retirement or paying for one's children's college education.

When images of material possessions, worry about paying bills, exotic vacations, or the latest fashions arise in our times of silence, we simply release these to God.

Sadness

The fourth distracting thought is sadness or deep distress. It's often an immobilizing sense of shame, guilt, and anxiety about our past and present. This is not necessarily a sin-driven sadness and it is not clinical depression. Rather it's a feeling of abandonment by God or others that leaves one with overwhelming feelings and images of depression and forlornness. These feelings may arise out of present challenges and/or hurts from the past.

I've encountered painful memories from early experiences in school to more recent episodes in my adult life. I've felt sadness over the pain that my children experienced during the divorce of their parents as well as the changes brought about in the aftermath. I've also experienced painful regret about many of my unrealized hopes and dreams.

Shame, guilt, and anxiety can easily manifest in thoughts such as *I'm not good enough, I don't do enough*, or *I don't have enough*. Although these feelings find their roots in our past experiences, the present or recent past can trigger them. One can be swamped by sadness during centering prayer, and it can be deeply distracting.

It may seem surprising that sitting in silence with God can bring forth these regrets and memories of unresolved pain. But it happens. The danger is that these sad thoughts easily pull us back into our thought stream and away from God. We watch old movies in our minds that create feelings of deep sadness. Yet we do not have to linger in times of melancholy. Instead, we simply return to our Lord.

Anger

The fifth distracting thought is anger. Bondi remarks that there is likely more written on the danger of anger in the monastic literature than on any of the other disordered emotions.[78] Anger is destructive both to others and to one's own soul. It creates long-term bitterness and resentment. If sadness is more internally focused, anger easily explodes outward. But anger is more than merely an external rage directed at the world. It can be more subtle.

In silence, we confront our internalized anger. I know this firsthand. I'm known as a level-headed nice guy. But silence has taught me that this is an illusion. It was a fake calm. My blood often boiled just under the surface. I simply had learned to keep a lid on it—*most of the time.*

When I first began centering prayer, I was confronted with thoughts of people who had wronged me in some way. I discovered that I'd created mental "hit lists." In other words, there were people from my past that I quietly hoped would "get theirs."

Evagrius described the effects of an anger-filled thought this way: "[It] renders the soul furious all day long, but especially during prayers it seizes the [mind] and represents to it the face of one who has distressed it."[79] For me it was not enough just to remember past events; I'd relive them. I'd cut loose on the perpetrators or I'd fantasize about the downfall of the person who hurt me. I'm not proud to confess this, but it's been part of my healing journey. In fact, recognizing the depths of my anger has helped me to grow in my ability and willingness to practice forgiveness and to be kinder and more compassionate to others.

When you discover yourself lost in anger, gently return to the silence with your prayer word. Surrendering thoughts of anger as they arise will slowly decompress the inner unconscious. Those around you will be grateful for the changes that they will see in you as you grow in your love for your neighbor.

Spiritual Sloth

The sixth distracting thought is sloth, but we need to reflect on its meaning carefully. This word is often the only word left untranslated from the original Greek that Evagrius used. *Acedia* is the ancient Greek term. Often *acedia* is translated with words such as "sloth," "listlessness" or "laziness." But these words miss the force of Evagrius's original counsel. Evagrius considered acedia to be particularly dangerous and called it the "noonday demon."

Acedia is not about general sloth or listlessness. It's not about having a bad day in which one doesn't pursue key tasks. It's more insidious. It's a deep-rooted despising of the present moment that constricts our faithfulness to the task at hand. Thus, I'm using the phrase "spiritual sloth" to distinguish it from mere laziness.

In the context of centering prayer, acedia involves inner thoughts such as: "Is this prayer session ever going to end?" or "What is the point of sitting here in silence? or "I can't wait for the timer to run out." Acedia is thus a thought about abandoning our commitments to sit in silence with God. It is a spiritual malaise.

How do we respond to acedia? The same way as with the others. When we catch ourselves in this thought, we surrender and return to the silence with our prayer word.

Vanity

Vanity is a compulsive desire for praise and recognition by others. As moderns, we are more likely to call this narcissism. It may also involve people-pleasing in order to be liked or admired by others.

In the context of centering prayer, vanity will manifest itself in thoughts about the praise one will receive from others for one's spirituality. Jesus gives three examples of this in Matthew 6:1–18. He critiques the public recognition of one's "works of righteousness" (alms to the poor, prayer, and fasting). He emphasizes the need to practice our spiritual habits in secret so that only God the Father knows about them. This is the antidote to vanity.

Vanity is a particular issue in our present day with the rise of social media. Whenever we become overly interested in how many likes or how much engagement we received for a post, we are in this realm. When we long for praise for our contribution to a particular ministry, we long for vanity. When we desire praise for our diligence and commitment to spiritual formation, we are looking for vanity.

When these types of thoughts arise in centering prayer, we have become too self-focused.

Pride

Pride is similar to vanity. If vanity is an obsession to gain praise and admiration, disordered pride is a focus on one's superiority over others. It is a distorted self-esteem that belittles and denigrates others.

Pride may creep into our centering prayer through thoughts of superiority or of our mastery of the practice. The supreme danger of pride is that it involves self-determination and idolatry. Not only am I better than others, but also I have attained a level of maturity in which I no longer need God's help. I've become the master of my destiny. I can rely on my personal resources and strategies to make my way through the world as a model of virtue and spiritual depth.

It may seem as though I'm overstating this temptation, but it is real. Centering prayer can make us feel as though we have found the "secret sauce" of the spiritual life. This can lead to thoughts of superiority over others. When these thoughts arise, know this: you are not receiving some confirmation about your growth from God. You are facing *pride*. Just as with the other "distracting" thoughts, there is a way forward.

Pressing Ahead

On the road to love, we will come to understand that these types of thoughts must be confronted in order to expand our capacity to love God, others, and self. Each of these thoughts serves as a roadblock to the depths of abundance that await the pilgrim willing to know the darkness on the way to the true light. Every time that one of these "demons" arises during the silence we learn to gently release it. This allows for deeper intimacy with God and opens up the gates for God's love to flow more freely into our souls.

Releasing these painful thoughts is like unclogging the plumbing of our inner world. When we surrender these thoughts to God, the pure water of God's love flows in. Or if we consider our inner world as a vast warehouse, time spent in the silence of centering prayer allows God to clear out the space presently occupied by our deep-seated hurts and struggles. The good news is that we now have room for the profound healing work of love that God desires for us.

Come Lord Jesus.

PART FOUR

Confronting the False Self

CHAPTER 14

The Enemy Within

"We have seen the enemy and he is us."
—POGO

There is an opponent who blocks us from loving in the ways that God desires. This adversary is likely not whom you suspect. It is not the devil or some evil force. In fact, it is not an external threat at all. The problem lies within. Psychologists and theologians call this our "false self." In the New Testament, Paul would call this the "old self" (Col. 3:9–10) or "life according to the flesh" (see Rom. 8:5).

The false self is our exalted self. In psychoanalytic terms, we may call it the "ego." It is the sum total of our experiences in the world, our acquired talents, and the defense mechanisms we've built since childhood to protect us and to help us to make it through life. It's the person each of us had to become in order to experience the love we craved. The false self includes strengths and talents as well as weaknesses and dark inclinations. We may think of our false self as the quintessential version of the American dream—a self-made person, pulled up by our bootstraps.

Underneath the false self lies the shadow part of our personality. Our shadow manifests in the world too, but it is more unconscious than conscious. The shadow represents the parts of us that we had to repress in public in order to find our place in the world. For every young person who is praised for being a "good boy" or "good girl," there is an inner "bad boy/bad girl" that simmers under the surface. For every strength, there is an underlying weakness or blind spot. The shadow manifests itself in the presence of certain triggers, stressors, or circumstances.

But the shadow also contains repressed talents and interests that we surrendered along the way. These didn't serve us in the pursuit of launching our career ambitions or in gaining the love we needed. For example, we may have given up music or creative writing or sports due to commitments to academics, training, or simply making a living.

Richard Rohr has written much on the false self, shadow, and true self. In *Immortal Diamond,* he summarizes four ways that our false self splits from and contrasts with who we truly are as persons loved deeply by God.[80] First, our false self masquerades as our real self at the cost of creating a repressed shadow. Second, life becomes centered in our thinking minds. We can lose touch with our essence. This means neglecting our true self as an embodied soul and not taking seriously our bodies, emotions, feelings, and thoughts. Third, the false self denies the presence of death and avoids it. Our denial of death may involve an overemphasis on the afterlife in our spirituality. Such a focus may result in the practice of religion as merely other-worldly rather than a moment-by-moment practice of the presence of God's love. We may fixate on heaven rather than learning to manifest God's love in our lives in the present. It can also lead in the opposite direction to the glorification of youthful vigor and beauty or the pursuit of eternal life through health or medicine. Last, the false self seeks to exist apart from others. Neighbors may become the suspicious "other" or even viewed as adversaries. Of course, isolation leads to broken relationships with our neighbor as well as with God.

Centering Prayer and the Work of God in Us

God desires to remake us in the image of Christ. This transforming work involves the full integration of all parts of ourselves through the work of the Spirit. There are various ways to talk about what this looks like. For example, Paul talks about the fruit of the spirit: love, joy, peace, patience, kindness, generosity, faithfulness, gentleness, and self-control (Gal. 5:22–23, cf. Col. 3:12–17). In essence, we live a life of love for God, for others, and for self.

The work of God in sanctification and renewal begins at the time of our conversion. It advances by God's grace gradually and at other times rapidly in deep moments of transformation. The main obstacle to transformation is our stubborn refusal to surrender ourselves fully to God.

Even if we consciously surrender a particular issue, thought, or struggle to God, our unconscious can still resist the work of the Spirit. I've experienced struggles that seem to confirm this. I've also observed, mentored, and counseled others who seemed stuck in deep-seated patterns of pain, victimhood, and sin. In other words, it is possible to experience authentic conversion and still distort the good news because of deeply held pain and beliefs that run counter to the Gospel.

In my tradition, we call unconscious negative behaviors *infirmities*. Infirmities include mistakes, misjudgments, and unintentional sins. On one hand, this is a helpful term because it maintains the need for believers to experience victory over *willful* or *conscious* sin. On the other hand, it gives us a pass on what I believe is a deeper work that God's grace can do over time.

In my reading of Scripture, I sense a profound optimism about the power of God's grace through the working of the Holy Spirit to change lives. In light of this, what if God's grace is capable of penetrating even the realm of our unconscious?

This is where centering prayer fits in. Thomas Keating talked about centering prayer as divine therapy.[81] The work of God produces love in our lives. One of the fruits of centering prayer is that God uses our time in silence to break down strongholds in us that prevent God's love from truly manifesting through us. This involves the work of confronting the false self and its shadow. It is here that the traditional language of dying to self is helpful. Gustave Reininger offers, "Indeed, the crucifixion of the false self is an ongoing process of purification facilitated and accelerated by centering prayer."[82]

Learning to love God, others, and yourself involves the integration of our conscious and unconscious parts. It is growth into the fullness of the person whom God created us to be. Jung called this *individuation*. Others may use the term "self-actualization." I like to think of it as wholeness in Christ. Or growth in grace.

This integration reveals our *true self*—the person who God created us to be. Our true self in Christ is the reintegration of our shadow with our false self in combination with the cleansing and empowerment of the Holy Spirit. Henri Nouwen describes this mode of living as the life of the beloved.[83] It is living as the object and subject of God's love without shame, guilt, or fear. We are loved by God, and we walk moment by moment in light of God's love and grace.

In *You are What You Love: The Power of Habit*, James K. A. Smith writes:

> We are what we want. Our wants and longings and desires are at the core of our identity, the wellspring from which our actions and behavior flow.[84]

The problem, Smith suggests, is that we may not love what we think we love and desire. This is a critical insight in our discussion of the false self. For Smith, the great danger for believers is not recognizing the forces and habits that influence our behaviors at the unconscious level.[85]

Many aspects of our lives run on autopilot. For example, we experience the unconscious when we drive along a familiar path and arrive at our destination with little memory of the trip. This is a relatively harmless function of the unconscious. But the problem is that our spirituality and capacity to love may be running on autopilot in ways contrary to the life that God truly desires for us.

So, how do we know what we truly love?

Self-Knowledge

I assume that you are interested in centering prayer because of your love for God and your desire to experience more of it in your life. By helping us to confront the reality of our false self and its shadow, centering prayer may guide us into ever-deepening levels of love for God, neighbor, and self.

Let me suggest something. We can assess what we love by how love manifests in our lives. For example, if I say that I love my wife, but engage in attitudes, behaviors, and actions that deny this, then I may need to question the sincerity of my love.

Scripture calls us to love the Lord with all that we are (intellect, will, emotions) in ways that produce the fruits of the Spirit. Jesus's command clearly suggests as much: "I give you a new commandment, that you love one another. Just as I have loved you, you also should love one another. By this everyone will know that you are my disciples, if you have love for one another" (John 13:34–35).

It seems, then, that the only way to assess the depth of our love is to observe the extent to which our lives produce results. Scripture calls these fruits of the Spirit. Fruitfulness is a metaphor that Scripture uses repeatedly. Psalm 1:3 describes the righteous person as one whose leaf never withers and whose fruit is always in season. In the Parable of the Soils (Matt. 13:1–9, 18–23), there are four soils, but only one of the four soils is fruitful and yields an abundant harvest.

Here is the radical problem: *What if I believe that I love the Lord and I embrace the faith but lack fruit or a sense of victory?*

In other words, I trust God deeply and receive the offer of God's unconditional love and grace through the life, death, and resurrection of Jesus. I seek to follow Jesus faithfully in response to his grace. I attend to the channels of grace that God provides. I read Scripture, pray, participate in Christian community and fellowship, attend worship including the celebration of the Lord's Supper, fast, serve the poor, and engage in evangelistic activities. This list is not intended to be a litmus test for faith or to be exhaustive. But it does include many of the common expectations for and practices of believers.

Yet what if my life produces little or no fruit? What if I struggle in relationships with others? What if I feel overwhelmed with feelings of guilt and shame that don't seem to have an obvious source? What if I believe that God loves others more than God loves me? What if, when I read texts such as Galatians 5:22–23—"the fruit of the Spirit is love, joy, peace, patience, kindness, generosity, faithfulness, gentleness, and self-control"—I lack some of these traits? Or they appear lacking in some glaring way despite my conscious surrender to Jesus Christ?

What if I experience hidden struggles with addictions to food, spending, or lust? What if I discover recurring relational patterns such as co-dependency or fears of trust/intimacy which make healthy friendships let alone intimate relationships difficult?

Flesh or Spirit?

Think about Paul's words in Romans 7:19: "For I do not do the good I want, but the evil I want is what I do." What if I identify with Paul's description?

What precisely is Paul even getting at in this verse? New Testament scholars debate Paul's intended meaning. Is Paul describing the norm for the Christian life? Or is Paul describing some pre-Christian version of a person? Or is Paul simply offering a word of grace to deeply sensitive persons who struggle with a tension between the promises of the Bible and their lived-out spirituality?

Regardless of the specifics, Paul in the following chapter, Romans 8, especially verses 1–17, emphasizes two critical lessons.

First, God provides the solution through the work of Jesus Christ. In Christ, there is "now no condemnation" (Rom. 8:1). Through Jesus Christ, we have experienced reconciliation with God, and there is no punishment forthcoming. God is not plotting our demise due to our struggles. Paul already made this clear a few chapters earlier. Romans 5:1 reads, "Therefore, since we are justified by faith, we have peace with God through our Lord Jesus Christ, through whom we have obtained access to this grace in which we stand; and we boast in our hope of sharing the glory of God." A few verses later Paul reminds us of God's action for us in Jesus Christ. "But God proves his love for us in that while we still were sinners Christ died for us" (Rom. 5:8).

Why are we seemingly digressing to the basics of the Gospel? Because we must embrace the reality that God is radically *for us*.

Our false self will always live in fear of rejection. Yet we don't have to cower or hide in the face of any inadequacies, guilt, or shame that we may feel. The journey to love is the discovery of the truth of God's love for us. We are accepted by God. We are enough for God. This is the gift of the Gospel through the faith of Jesus Christ. The deep work that God does through centering prayer helps to make the grace of God a felt reality in our lives.

Second, Paul does not leave us stuck in patterns of defeat. In Romans 8, he teaches us that the work of the Holy Spirit empowers us to rise above our flesh. "Flesh" (Greek: *sarx*) is a misunderstood concept in Paul. It is often translated as "sinful nature." According to this reading, the flesh is the part of us that causes us to sin. There is a kernel of truth here, but it overstates the power of the flesh.

To live by the flesh is to place ultimate reliance on our human resources apart from God's grace. In other words, to live by the flesh is to live solely out of the strengths of our false self with its shadow. It is to depend on ourselves in order to make it through the world.

Let me illustrate what it would mean for you to live by the flesh. Ask yourself: When I am placed into a difficult situation, to what do I turn? Does my ability to make it through the world depend on my intellect, gifts, and talents? When we live and act as if success and failure depend fully on our resources, we live by the flesh.

When I face a struggle in my life, my mind goes into hyperdrive. I try to formulate a plan or strategy to overcome the challenge before me. Before you say, "Well, that makes sense!" or "What is wrong with that?" Let me say, the danger of self-reliance is that we may act as if there were no God or grace or bigger reality.

The truth is that you and I have tangible gifts and talents. All people do. This blessing is also a danger. Our greatest strengths can become our most glaring weaknesses. For it is often directly beneath our strengths that the shadow and false self operate.[86] Thus, it is our flesh that needs the influx of God's grace continually. Living by the flesh is a denial of our need for grace. It is the illusion that we can control our destiny.

Paul describes the need to live by the Holy Spirit. This means learning to rely and live in dependence on a reality much bigger than our limited gifts, talents, resources, and drives. He promises a lot:

> If Christ is in you, though the body is dead because of sin, the Spirit is life because of righteousness. If the Spirit of him who raised Jesus from the dead dwells in you, he who raised Christ from the dead will give life to your mortal bodies also through his Spirit that dwells in you. So then, brothers and sisters, we are debtors, not to the flesh, to live according to the flesh—for if you live according to the flesh, you will die; but if by the Spirit you put to death the deeds of the body, you will live. (Rom. 8:10–13)

For Paul, the antidote to the temptation to live as if everything depends on our resources of self, family, and community is radical dependence on the Spirit.

Embrace the Silence through Surrender

Living by the Spirit sounds easy enough. But it isn't. For the challenge is this: we can mute the work of the Spirit with our conscious and unconscious actions, thoughts, and beliefs.

Rohr writes of the blocks to God's grace caused by our self-talk: "If this inner and critical voice has kept you safe for many years as your inner voice of authority, you may end up not being able to hear the real voice of God."[87] Our false self is strong. It is the young child within us who at the moment of her wounding begins to live with a clenched fist. She feels the angst of not being enough and overcompensates by striving to become better, stronger, and faster. She begins to struggle to be the captain of the ship. As Paul suggests, our false self is metaphorically hell-bound in its attempt.

Our false self is also weak. It is the adult whose childhood or adolescent wounds pierced him deeply enough that the pain is crippling. It sucked the confidence and joy out of him. Out of the depths of the soul arises melancholy, anxiety, and fear of the world. As with Eeyore from *Winnie the Pooh*, dark clouds hover over life. Many may experience life as a series of misfortunes. We become stuck and carry the weight of victimhood. We are already living in a hell of sorts.

Both the strong and weak dimensions are hidden albatrosses that we wear in the flesh. These aspects of ourselves mute the work of the Spirit. For the self-reliant, the flesh overcompensates for our sense of lack. I fall into this category. I have pushed myself from adolescence to prove my worth. I competed with classmates to have the highest GPA and test scores. I so desired the approval of my teachers that I sometimes sacrificed my natural curiosity and made their research interests my own. It wasn't enough to work one job when I could work two or more. I loved being known as a "workhorse" and judged others for being lazy or not "on mission." At home, I strove to be the "good" son, a "great husband," an "all-star dad." At work, I pushed myself to be an "award-winning and innovative teacher" and "entrepreneurial-minded administrator." As far as my commitment to Jesus Christ,

I was "all in" and a "true believer." All this was great in my life until it wasn't.

For the self-defeated, the flesh grips the shame and hurt from our wounds so tightly that it becomes their identity. Many walk through life in a state of perpetual sadness. They keep the blinds of their inner world pulled down to keep out any light. They are God's "frozen chosen." They feel the lack of not being enough, but instead of fighting tooth and nail, they surrender before the rising tides of life.

When we open ourselves to the work of the Spirit, the flesh is defenseless. Yet we erect barriers to the work of God. With our mouths we sing of God's "Amazing Grace," but deep inside our unconscious we resonate more with a karaoke version of Sinatra's "My Way." This is true of both the strong, the weak, and those in between. The Spirit stands at the door knocking, but we must open the door to our inner control panel. This means surrendering our strengths, talents, and passions and our weaknesses, wounds, and fears.

I've found that centering prayer serves as an antidote to our conscious and unconscious blocking of the Spirit's work in our lives. By our sitting in silence and surrendering our thoughts, God will slowly break open our unconscious patterns. When these surface we follow the 4 Rs: resist no thought, retain no thought, react to no thought, return gently to our sacred word. This simple process opens us up to substantial healing through the grace, mercy, and love of God.

CHAPTER 15

Entering the Cave

"Oh God, help me to believe the truth about myself, no matter
how beautiful it is."

—SR. MACRINA WIEDERKEHR[88]

In the film *Star Wars (Episode 5): The Empire*

Strikes Back, there is an iconic scene in which Jedi Master Yoda
trains Luke by sending him into a cave. In this dreamlike sequence,
Luke encounters his potential dark side in the form of the Sith
Lord Darth Vader. In a battle inside this cave, Luke kills Vader.
He removes Vader's mask only to see his own face. So it is, when
we face our false self. Yet it is in the process of knowing our inner
darkness that we discover the deepest truths about ourselves.

Facing the truth is the hard part. Who really wants to explore
the depths of one's soul, especially the wounded and frightened
parts? Rohr writes, "No one oversees his or her own demise
willingly, even when it is the false self that is dying."[89]

How does one enter the cave to begin to experience the love
of God and confront the false self? Centering prayer is one
pathway that I've found helpful. Centering prayer invites us to
surrender in silence before God. Bourgeault describes the path as
"the gathering awareness that the cave of the heart is entered not
only or even primarily through purification and concentration,
but through surrender and release."[90]

There is no great work on our part. We cannot earn access to
our inner regions. Our sole contribution is the surrender of every
thought to God.

So what makes the confrontation of the false self so unsettling? It's simple. Most of us prefer and are accustomed to a more unexamined life. Our default is to see the faults of others without the self-awareness of our own.

Yet if we want to be of true service to others, we have to look deeply into our inner world. Jesus knew this and taught:

Why do you see the speck in your neighbor's eye, but do not notice the log in your own eye? Or how can you say to your neighbor, "Let me take the speck out of your eye," while the log is in your own eye? You hypocrite, first take the log out of your own eye, and then you will see clearly to take the speck out of your neighbor's eye. (Matt. 7:3–5)

When we take a deep dive and face our shadow persona, we will discover both hidden treasures and skeletons. Self-awareness demands that we peer at both. The treasures and skeletons are often bound tightly together. They are not easily separated.

In the movie *The Lord of the Rings: The Twin Towers*, Théodan king of Rohan is under the evil influence of the sorcerer Saruman via a powerful spell. When we first meet him, Théodan is a weak and withered old man who has abdicated his responsibility to fight for the good of his people. We may say metaphorically that he is controlled by his false self. Yet the true self still abides in Théodan. When the wizard Gandalf arrives in the throne room, he immediately sees the truth and uses his power to free Théodan from the inner demons afflicting him. Théodan transforms back to his true self: a heroic, strong, middle-aged, warrior king with a heart for his people and his land. He becomes a major force for good in the struggle against the evil of Saruman and in *The Lord of the Rings: The Return of the King* against the forces of Sauron of Mordor.

This is a powerful metaphor for the work that God can do in our lives through liberating grace. Centering prayer is one of the means that God can use to penetrate the darkness within us. In silence, we can experience both our inner darkness and the seeds of the person God created us to be. God doesn't leave us to our own devices and strength to sort these out.

Who will save us from the darkness? What do we do when confronted with the truth about ourselves? In response to this self-knowledge, we join the desert fathers and mothers of ages past who prayed by following the model of the Pharisee in Luke 18:13—"Lord Jesus Christ, Son of God, have mercy on me, a sinner."

Then, we listen to the Psalmist who prayed, "Taste and see that the LORD is good; happy are those who take refuge in him" (Ps. 34:8).

When we become aware of the false self, we lose the illusion of our goodness. The moments in which we learn deeper truths about ourselves may be startling. We recognize our deep brokenness even subsequent to our previous experiences of God's grace. We become acutely mindful of our ongoing moment-by-moment need for God's grace and love.

The challenge of life is recognizing that all other options are counterfeit solutions. These counterfeit solutions grip us because they soothe our pain. They allow us to avoid feeling the depth of our hurt. Part of the power of centering prayer is that in the silence we may sit in conscious recognition, perhaps for the first time, of what has been hidden deep within. This is the beginning of the work of the Spirit in our lives.

Thanks be to God!

CHAPTER 16

Healing of the False Self

"Solitude is the furnace of transformation."
—HENRI NOUWEN[91]

Our core wounding manifests in the false self with its shadow. Deep fears of being abandoned and overwhelmed reside in the recesses of our souls. Whether we are aware or not, most of us live bouncing between these two fears.

The fear of abandonment creates a sense of lack. We feel a nagging ache that we are not enough. We are not good enough. We are not doing enough. We feel guilt, shame, and fear.

We believe that if only we can prove ourselves through action, performance, and results, we will earn all of the love that we need. The irony is that this puts us into the throes of being overwhelmed. We heroically take on too much work. We attempt to live as the ideal son, daughter, friend, wife, husband, lover, colleague, boss, and/or whatever other role we embrace.

But what happens when we do all of the right things yet still feel the lack? We then find ourselves doubly distressed and anxious. In those moments, we turn to whatever stress-relieving activities give us a moment's respite.

This can even include religious practices. Religion can undermine our actual healing when it's rooted in views of God that merely reflect the worst of our wounds rather than the true beauty of God. This is idolatry. Religion then functions as a constricting ideology rather than a liberating reality. This is the god who always demands more. If we are deeply wounded, we may misuse expressions of commitment such as "It's my cross to bear" or "It was my duty" or "I did it for the sake of the gospel and God's kingdom." We may "count the cost" and wear it as a badge of honor.

The fear of being overwhelmed also derives from a sense of lack. Early in life we may feel a lack of love from significant persons when we need it most. We learn that we are not always lovable, and that the world can be a frightening place. We sometimes feel that "I am not enough" or "I don't deserve love" or, even worse, "I am worthless." These wounds can drive us to find nurture, acceptance, and love at all costs. This leads to unbalanced relationships and in the worse situations outright abuse. The hunger for love slowly constricts the soul's health.

Religion and Our Wounds

Our religious commitments ironically may have served to further enmesh us with a false identity. We became the victim whom God rescued or the worm whom God redeemed.

Hear me carefully: *God does redeem.* This is the heart of the gospel. What follows is not a dismissal of the gospel. The point is: God wants to do an even more profound work than we imagine. God wants to heal us in the depths of our being so that we are freed to live as his missional people for the sake of the world.

God desires to liberate us from all the chains that bind us. Jesus died on the cross for our sins, our shame, our pain, every injustice we've committed or experienced, our diseases, our weaknesses, and our infirmities. Through the gospel, God is at work in us "making all things new."[92]

But the false self presents a danger at any moment in which God breaks into our life. If the shadow remains strong, the wound of neediness may manifest itself in the pursuit of continual "saving moments." The fear of being overwhelmed and the need to compensate by finding love may drive some to chase one spiritual experience after another. For others it means living as a person whose life is a perpetual prayer request, full of pain and suffering. They identify solely with their status as a victim. We sometimes lionize such individuals in our communities of faith for their perseverance in suffering. Yes, there are individuals who through no fault of their own suffer from poor DNA, accidents, and chronic illness. We've all known dear saints whose testimonies declare the power of faith and the love of God in truly difficult circumstances. Yet entire communities of faith exist in melancholic states of pain and woundedness.

My Cautionary Tale

I struggled to fit in once I hit adolescence. I was not prepared for the bullying and humiliations of middle school. My "good boy" nature along with my shy awkwardness made me easy pickings. I learned quickly that I was not enough. I experienced real pain. I was placed ahead of my peers into advanced courses in both seventh and eighth grade. The other students were almost all a full grade ahead of me. This was compounded by a late birthday in the school year. This meant that I was in class with some students who were eighteen months to two years more mature than I. This was too much for a twelve-year-old. My strong intellect did not compensate socially for my lack of maturity and emotional intelligence. These two years were full of embarrassment and shame. By my ninth-grade year, I achieved a new persona. I was then one of the oldest in the school. Most of my former tormentors were in high school. I shifted from being a "good boy" to putting on the mask of a "bad boy" or at least as "bad" as I could be for a naive young man raised in the church. This persona only lasted about a year.

This set me up for a dramatic conversion experience in the spring of my tenth-grade year. I began attending my church's youth fellowship that school year. I joined the youth program primarily because there were girls who actually showed me attention. Not the best reason, but also not an uncommon one!

We had several caring youth leaders, but I gravitated to Steve. Steve was about thirty years old at the time. He was a brilliant mathematician who worked for Goodyear Tire and Rubber Company. He was our Bible teacher and he loved Scripture. I respected him one hundred percent because in him I saw an intellect that impressed me. He was smart and he believed in God. At a New Year's Eve celebration, Steve challenged us to read Scripture for ourselves in the coming year. A couple of months later, I was still deeply floundering in my life, so I picked up my Bible in my bedroom and prayed, "Lord, if you are real, reveal yourself to me." A few weeks later, I had a classic conversion experience. At a revival service, I answered the altar call given by the evangelist, walked down the aisle, and gave my life to Jesus.

From that moment until my divorce twenty-six years later, faith was the central focus of my life. It still is today, but it's different. Looking back, I can see how my conversion answered my wound of abandonment.

Faith in Jesus Christ rooted in the study of the Bible provided certainty in my life. Moreover, the countercultural underpinnings of the gospel allowed me to reboot my outsider status at school into something I proudly owned as proof of my conversion. I gained esteem and respect from peers for the strength of my convictions. I also earned the attention of adults, including my pastor who mentored me and encouraged me regarding the ministry. I felt significant and loved.

But this also created a darker pattern. It wasn't enough to live a life of grace. I had to be "all in." I wanted to be counted among the saints. I responded readily to messages about the dramatic calls of missionaries and pastors. I resonated with the exhortations to sacrificial living. But this drove me directly into the teeth of the other great fear: feelings of being overwhelmed. My desires to prove myself sent me into self-defeating patterns of overwork to compensate for my sense of lack and my inability to accept the truth that I was unconditionally accepted.

My story illustrates one of Thomas Keating's emphases about the need for deep cleansing at the level of our unconscious. By deep cleansing, I'm referring to times when God's grace confronts our false self. Without it, religion simply becomes part of the problem. Keating writes:

> If we do not recognize and confront the hidden influences of the emotional programs for happiness, the false self will adjust to any new situation in a short time and nothing is really changed. If we enter the service of the Church, the symbols of security, success, and power in the new milieu will soon become the objects of our desires.[93]

Our wounding can mask selfishness by appearing selfless and thus Christlike. The difference between a wound-driven self-centeredness and a Christ-inspired other-centeredness is not easily spotted in our lives apart from deep self-awareness. A lifestyle of selfless living emerges out of love, but fear manifests in selfishness. When love is the true driver, we find key markers present: joy, gratitude, hope, truth, generosity, and calmness. When fear sits in our inner engine room, we find bitterness, passive-aggressive behavior, clinginess, and neediness, along with a sense of lack, anxiety, guilt, and shame.

Such times are when centering prayer may do its deepest work. Sitting in silent meditative prayer allows God to show us our true wounds. When we experience these moments, they can prove tantamount to watching a mountain move before our eyes.

When we sit in silence, we slowly relax into God's presence. This puts us into a physical state where our unconscious can surface, and we can see our deepest wounds and points where we are stuck.

In the presence of God in silence, our flesh can be astonished by the experience of God's love. In the nakedness of the moment, the truth of unconditional acceptance calls out to us. This is grace. This is the work of the Spirit. This is the moment of passing from dependence on the flesh to an openness to the Spirit's power to heal and transform us. We consciously release the truth of who we are into the loving embrace of the Spirit.

Many of us struggle with assurance. The practice of centering prayer may be a vehicle for gaining the experience that Paul describes in Romans. It may facilitate our surrender in God's presence so that God's Spirit may sing in concert with our own about our acceptance:

"It is that very Spirit bearing witness with our spirit that we are children of God. . ." (Rom. 8:16).

CHAPTER 17

Breaking Through
to the True You

"How we view ourselves at any given moment may have
very little to do with who we really are."
—GERALD MAY[94]

The good news is that each of us is a person
whom God loves deeply and for whom God desires our best.
The bad news is that this truth is often buried beneath layers of
ideology, bad theology, pop psychology, and deep wounds that
have left hardened scar tissue.

In my practice of centering prayer, I've confronted my inner
demons. Or more precisely they've confronted me. Rather than
casting them out, I've learned to love them because they were not
a foreign invader.

Centering prayer helped me to observe and confront my full
self without shame or judgment. I've slowly begun to love myself
for the sake of God. To talk about growth in love for myself may
seem odd, given what I've shared so far about my shadow, but
this is only because we've lost sight of the deep love that God has
for us. As we saw, God is holy love. God is the loving father who
desires deep intimacy with his daughters and sons. Moreover, this
loving father desires our best, and so God's love is also a light that
illuminates and purifies the darkness.

This is not about reveling in sin in order to magnify God's
grace. God does not need magnification. God is magnificent on

God's own. Neither my best nor my worst enhances or diminishes God's love for me.

Confronting the Darkness

The gospel assumes our substantial transformation by God's grace. But this expectation of transformation can feel oppressive under the weight of lingering sin. These feelings of oppression derive from a stance before God of fear and shame. We forget that God's grace is the catalyst, not our efforts. History is strewn with extreme actions of saints in pursuit of victory through acts of the will.

Centering prayer slowly teaches us a way of loving ourselves for the sake of God. When we sit in silence and surrender our thoughts, we open ourselves intimately and fully to the God who loves us. In fact, centering prayer can be a catalyst for identifying deep-rooted patterns of sin—the ones hiding in the shadows. In the process, we learn to love ourselves—even our repressed shadow.

This process can be troubling, but I am profoundly optimistic about the gospel's power in breaking sinful patterns in our lives and substantially transforming us through God's grace.

Richard Rohr's words are helpful:

Our mistakes are something to be pitied and healed much more than hated, denied, or perfectly avoided. I do not think you should get rid of your sin until you have learned what it has to teach you. Otherwise, it will only return in new forms, as Jesus says of the "unclean spirit" that returns to the house all "swept and tidied" (Luke 11:24–26); then he rightly and courageously says that "the last state of the house will be worse than the first."[95]

When I first read those words, I recoiled from the idea that sin had something to teach me. But as I pondered it more, I began to grasp Rohr's point. We tend to suppress what we deny. Our sins are an affront to God's holiness. They represent all of the manifold ways we miss the mark, willingly transgress, and demonstrate our lostness. We need God's grace. When we recognize the truth about ourselves, the ancient prayer of confession flows easily from our lips:

Most merciful God,
we confess that we have sinned against you
in thought, word, and deed,
by what we have done,
and by what we have left undone.
We have not loved you with our whole heart;
We have not loved our neighbors as ourselves.

Centering prayer enhances our sense of lostness, but it also gives us a different perspective on our sins. We can observe them in a detached way from the position of surrender. As we sit in silence, the opening of our being before God includes a full display of our inner life: memories, desires, dreams, anxieties, points of stress, emotional wounds, and yes, even our core lostness. Don't mistake what I'm saying here: I'm not glorifying patterns of sin or suggesting that we are missing out on important lessons unless we have engaged in sinful practices. Surely this is not the case. But our sins can teach us about our inner depths from which these sins emerge. Augustine hinted at the same idea when commenting on Romans 8:28, "All things work together for good for those who love God," by adding "even our sins."[96]

Each sin is its own iceberg. The sinful practice is the part we act out in our lives. It is the concrete and specific way in which we fail to love God and neglect the love of our neighbors. But under every sin is its true root. It emerges from our inner swampland. Christians often call this our "sin nature." It stems from a deep brokenness and doubt that God has our best interests at heart.

Learning to See Ourselves as God Sees Us

Now I'm not suggesting that centering prayer is a pathway to absolute perfection. Nor am I imagining a state in this life in which we are one hundred percent free from the human propensity to sin. If Scripture teaches anything, it is this truth: "All have sinned and fall short of the glory of God" (Rom. 3:23). John amplifies this in 1 John 1:8, "If we say that we have no sin, we deceive ourselves, and the truth is not in us"; and 1:10, "If we say that we have not sinned, we make him a liar, and his word is not in us." Yet the profound confrontation with the roots of sin opens us to the tremendous possibility of authentic transformation.

Charles Wesley captured this lyrically in his "O for a Thousand Tongues to Sing" when he penned,

> He breaks the power of cancell'd sin,
> He sets the prisoner free;
> His blood can make the foulest clean;
> His blood avail'd for me.

Wesley grasped the optimism of what God's grace can do in our lives. Yet how many of us still live under the power of "cancelled" sin? We recognize that we've been forgiven, but do we agree with Wesley's belief that God's grace is capable of getting to the root?

This idea may make some readers uncomfortable. Let me be clear. I am not suggesting "sinless perfection" or anything close to that. We will always need the grace of God regardless of the depths to which God's grace penetrates our being. Thus, our relationship with God is grounded in deep trust and dependence.

When we recognize the profound love of God for us, we experience new freedoms. We are free from the need to pull ourselves up by our bootstraps. We are free from needing to perform to have value, acceptance, or love. We recognize the immensity of God's grace. God's grace then becomes the empowering force in our life.

Our goal is growth in the three loves: love for God, love for neighbor, and love for self. When we talk about breaking the power of sin, it is critical to remember this goal. The goal is not avoidance of sin, but the increase in our capacity for love. Sin constricts our ability to love. As sin loses its grip, love flows freely and bears fruit.

The question for us then is, can the grace of God through the work of the Spirit break open and heal some of the deep-rooted causes of our sins? I believe the answer is yes. But we have to see and then confess them consciously by presenting them as an offering to the Lord. To use Rohr's language, we need to learn from our sins. This means receiving not merely God's forgiveness but also God's deep cleansing.

As I've sat quietly before God in centering prayer, I've seen parts of myself that I wished weren't there. I've watched thoughts of anger, lust, humiliation, shame, pain, disappointment, and guilt float by. Episodes from my past that I'd prefer never happened replay in my thoughts. But when I release these gently with the sacred word, Jesus abides with me. I experience God's loving presence, and this allows me to offer my sins and wounds for a deep cleansing.

But there is more. When we begin to see ourselves as God does, illusions about motives slip away. Instead, we see clearly our actual desires and wants. All of this occurs in the presence of God. My wounds appear. Some are self-inflicted. Some are the result of the intentional and unintentional acts of others. Some are inherited and embedded in my genetic makeup. They all slowly emerge in centering prayer. I then surrender them in the presence of God. I sit in silence knowing that I am fully known by God. Abiding in this sacred space is how God slowly heals me and breaks the bonds that prevent me from living as the person I was created to be—a person who loves God, neighbor, and self and continues to grow in these loves.

"To put it another way," Rohr writes, "what I let God see and accept in me also becomes what I can then see and accept in myself. And even more, it becomes that whereby I see everything else. This is 'radical grace.'"[97]

Loving Yourself for the Sake of God

As we draw near in silence to the one who draws near to us, we can finally gaze into our soul and smile. We can hear the chatter within. We can observe the film of our past or future lives created by thoughts. We can experience the emotions stored on our inner hard drives. Regardless, moment by moment we release our attachment to all of these in surrender with our sacred word.

The gentle return to God with our sacred word changes everything. In silent surrender, we discover that we are not alone in the journey. We have a companion who knows us. We have a companion who died for us. We have a companion who loves us.

The story of the prodigal son offers us a choice. Will we receive the astonishingly lavish love of God in the full recognition of who we are (as the prodigal did) or will we storm off in protest as the older son did? Of course, there is only one sensible choice. Rohr puts it this way:

> Your work is of another kind: to stay calmly and happily on the road and not get back into the harness. St. Teresa of Avila used a similar metaphor when she described how you can either keep digging the channel or find the actual spring and let it just flow toward you, in you and from you.[98]

This is the beauty of the process of centering prayer. We experience God's love for us. Its unconditional nature is astonishing. It frees us to see ourselves as we are: *a mixed bag of brokenness and woundedness interwoven with the potential of living fully as persons crafted in God's image.* Then we can look at others: both their deepest flaws *and* their potential as the person that God created them to be. This reframing of encounters with others is the process of growth in grace.

CHAPTER 18

The Upward Spiral of Love

"How you love is how you have accessed love."
—RICHARD ROHR[99]

When I truly believe the truth about myself

(good and bad), I have learned to love myself as the person that God created me to be. And since I love myself, I can now love God more profoundly. I can sing Charles Wesley's words with a whole heart: "Amazing love, how can it be that thou my God shouldst die for me?" and "'Tis mercy all, immense and free; For, O my God, it found out me."[100]

Through centering prayer, I see myself as God sees me without recoiling in shame, guilt, or fear. My false self and shadow lose power, and the real me with my strengths and weaknesses emerges for the sake of and glory of God. My interactions with others find their roots in this love too.

I can love God with my heart, soul, and strength. This may sound boastful, but stick with me. As I've said previously, I am not talking about absolute perfection. We are talking about relationships, not mathematical precision. There will always be areas of growth. This is the beauty of love.

To use a biblical metaphor, consider the opening stories of creation. In Genesis, God makes a "very good" world (Gen. 1:31). He crafts humanity in his image and commissions humanity to fill the earth and rule over it in the sense of serving as stewards of its goodness (1:28). This is the calling of our lives. We serve as God's ambassadors to the rest of creation. In Genesis 2:4–25, the narrative shifts to the garden of Eden. Genesis 2:15 clarifies the mission of humanity as existing to "serve and keep [the garden]" (translation mine). This does not suggest that Adam and Eve's vocation was to spend eternity merely preserving the garden as is. They were not mere caretakers. Instead, the language of "serving and keeping" suggests creative engagement and improvement of the garden.

How does one improve a garden? It would certainly involve the pruning of older plants and less healthy shoots for the greater good of the whole. It may mean moving shrubbery or introducing new types of seed into the garden. In other words, we are talking about enhancing and cultivating an already good garden. So it is with love. Once we open ourselves to love we enter an ever-flowing stream that carries us in ever deepening understandings and experiences of love divine.

What does this deepening look like? Since I no longer hide from or am ignorant of my false self, I am free to love and be loved. My inner bent to self-rule and sin are in the open. I am less a slave of many gods, and I can more deeply live out the truth that the Lord is "my one and only." The response to knowing Jesus as "my one and only" is whole-person love. This capacity to love continues to grow.

Then I can love others more profoundly because my heart beats more regularly with the heartbeat of God's love for the world. To experience God's grace, forgiveness, and compassion in spite of the truth about myself has changed the way that I can see others. One of my mentors, Bob Tuttle, once instructed me to pray, "Lord, help me to see others as though they were my own children." Of course, this assumes you actually like your children! Tuttle's goal was to create pathways for others to see with God's eyes. The deep practice of centering prayer has changed the way

I think about this advice. "Lord, help me to see others in the same way that I've learned to know myself in light of your lavish love."

Thomas Merton writes:

> It is in deep solitude that I find the gentleness with which I can truly love my brothers. The more solitary I am the more affection I have for them. . . . Solitude and silence teach me to love my brothers for what they are, not for what they say.[101]

Slowly I find myself being more patient with others. I am a little slower to judge others because I've received God's unconditional acceptance for my greater offenses. Jesus's warning about casting judgment in Matthew 7:1–5 takes on new meaning. It no longer seems hyperbolic to speak of taking a log out of my own eye before helping a neighbor with their speck. I am becoming a student of others rather than a teacher and judge. What can I learn from the other? When I catch myself moving to judgment, I turn it on myself and ponder the reasons for my reaction. I feel greater moments of compassion.

Last, I can love myself more profoundly for the sake of God. The old lyric, "Jesus loves me, this I know, for the Bible tells me so" is a wonderful song, but I now know God's love *experientially* and not merely intellectually. Scripture's promises now take on new meaning in deep meditative prayer in which I've felt in moments and spied in glimpses the immensity of God's love for even me.

I've become a wounded healer. My wounds, once buried deep within my soul, have been revealed. What God has shown me in centering prayer about myself has changed me. This change is the result of God's unconditional love for me despite my brokenness, pain, and sin. God did not turn away when I'd have preferred to hide in shame. The experience of grace, compassion, and forgiveness of ourselves liberates us so that our wounds may in fact become signs of hope for others.

This is a critical move. When we shift from a fear-, guilt-, and shame-based existence to one of acceptance and love, we open more fully to the world. Our story morphs from a novella rooted in the false self to a fully nuanced autobiography that reveals the true depths of our existence and explores every facet of our character. This is not without risk, of course. It feels uncomfortable and vulnerable to share my story. But God writes a story of grace-filled renewal not as an end in itself. Every experience of God's grace is a commission to mission.

In my ministry as a professor, I share my knowledge of Scripture and theology with my students. But I also share myself. I no longer fear pulling back the curtain on my soul. I maintain healthy boundaries, but I do try to give students a glimpse into my past and the ways that God has brought profound healing into my life through his love and grace in centering prayer.

This sharing of my woundedness has served as permission for students to engage me outside of class for spiritual direction and counsel. One student remarked, "The way you handled yourself in class talking so openly yet sensitively about yourself signaled to me that you were a safe person worthy of my trust." Over the past few years, I've had as much impact in rich conversations about formation outside of the classroom as I've had through teaching theology inside the classroom.

There is something ironic about our wounds becoming visible. They actually help others rather than repel them. Our false self screams, "Don't let others see the real you!" But we have a savior who remains the "crucified one." Jesus's resurrected form did not erase the signs of his crucifixion. If anything, it amplified their power. Famously in John's Gospel, Thomas struggled to believe that Jesus was risen from the dead (John 20:24–29). Thomas found certainty when Jesus appeared to him and invited Thomas to touch his nail-scarred hands and spear-pierced side. Thomas then cried out, "My Lord and my God!"

Learning to love ourselves means loving our wounds and allowing them to be marks not of shame but of love divine. As wounded healers we become ambassadors of the Risen Christ (the crucified one) who will meet us in love and mercy. We may find that we too have wounds that heal.

PART FIVE

The Fruits
of Centering Prayer

CHAPTER 19

Into the World

"To live by faith, to be known by love, and to be a voice of hope."
—ERWIN MCMANUS [102]

In this chapter and the ones that follow,

to conclude, we will explore some of the fruits of centering prayer in daily life. The purpose of centering prayer is to sit in silence in the presence of the God who loves us. But over time practitioners will manifest real change in their lives because every experience of God's love and grace is transformational.

Reentry When Prayer Ends

The moment you open your eyes you reenter the present world. The stillness of the silence drifts away. But is it possible to carry into daily life the depth of contemplation we discovered in centering prayer?

This is the work of living in the world as an ambassador of God's love. Keating focuses on two components to carry forward our time of prayer into our work and family settings.[103]

First, we must set our *attention* to the matters at hand. We shift from being present with God in solitude to being present in our relationships and work. If I am conversing with my spouse or child, then I give them my full attention. I consciously release any distracting thought so that I can listen to them. Likewise, as I write this paragraph, I focus on communicating with you, my reader.

Second, I pay attention because I have set the *intention* of my action: I am loving God in all that I do. This is the "why" or purpose. In the process, I practice being in the presence of God. The love God has shown to me in meditative prayer manifests itself in small ways moment by moment throughout the day. Brother Lawrence writes, "We ought not to be weary of doing little things for the love of God, who regards not the greatness of the work, but the love with which it is performed."[104] My mentor and friend Bob Tuttle often gives this advice for living for God in the world: "Show up. Pay attention. God has more invested in this than you do."

Centering prayer teaches us to surrender our thoughts to God. The same practice can continue in our daily lives. Set the same intention to treat the time with the person in front of you as you do when you sit in silence before God in centering prayer. Remember that we are not merely our thoughts. We are more than the narrative, soundtrack, or film running through our minds. Release your thought loops and pay attention to whoever or whatever is at hand.

Is it possible to live this way consistently? It depends what we mean by consistently. If we mean staying fully present at all times, I'm not there, but this does not mean that we stop trying or stop practicing daily centering prayer. Every time we pray, it is a matter of bringing our attention back to the present moment and to the task in which we are involved. Deny self. Take up the cross. Follow Jesus into the world. When I find I'm distracted, I realign with the work of the moment and do it for the love of God.

Keating calls this *contemplative service*. It is profoundly missional. The gospel encounters us on its way to someone else. Keating observes, "Complete submission to God allows the divine energy to radiate and others seeing this have a sense of being in touch with God or in the midst of a community where love exists."[105] Is this not what each soul longs for? Is this not what our world is desperate to experience?

In the Gospel of Luke, the familiar story of Martha and Mary (Luke 10:38–42) serves as an illustration of the tension of remaining in the now while seeking to serve. In this story, Jesus is teaching in Martha's home at her invitation. Martha's sister, Mary, sits at Jesus's feet in order to listen to him. Martha, however, is distracted by her many tasks—presumably, the need to care for guests. She is committed to assuming responsibility for others. She complains to Jesus that Mary is not helping her. Instead of being sympathetic, Jesus responds, "Martha, Martha, you are worried and distracted by many things; there is need of only one thing. Mary has chosen the better part, which will not be taken away from her" (Luke 10:41–42). This story has levels of richness, but I want to use it as a metaphor for centering prayer and its connection to the busy-ness of life. It would be wrong to denigrate Martha for having a desire to serve. The issue is her distractedness. She likely wanted to *hear* Jesus, as well, but she prioritized working over focused time with God. Mary modeled a life of focused presence with Jesus. She understood gender roles at the time regarding service, but she privileged the opportunity to sit at Jesus's feet.

By learning to be present with Jesus moment by moment we fill ourselves with God's riches and love. This filling prepares us for loving service in the world for others. When we read about Martha and Mary, the text is not calling us to an either/or of time with God or service of others. Instead, it is about reprioritizing. Teresa of Avila wrote, "Martha and Mary must join together . . . desire and be occupied in prayer not for the sake of our enjoyment but so as to have this strength to serve."[106] Centering prayer is a propellant for us to show up fully, moment by moment, in our daily habits and lives.

Living the Mission

I often suggest to my students that they pray, "Lord, who is my mission?" This is the sort of prayer that God answers. The key is whether or not we are listening. In his sublime *Life Together*, Dietrich Bonhoeffer speaks of the need to allow ourselves to be interrupted by God. God will always send people our way. We will be tempted to assert our plans and timetables over their needs. But, Bonhoeffer writes, "When we do that we pass by the visible sign of the Cross raised athwart our path to show us that, not our way, but God's way must be done."[107] The person who is fully present must hold loosely to his or her schedule to make room for the needs in the moment of another.

In the novel *The Shack*, the protagonist Mack encounters the Triune God at the same park where his daughter was abducted and murdered by a serial killer. He experiences profound healing, including a vision of his daughter safe and secure with God. When it is time for Mack to return home, Mack is offered the choice to stay with God forever. He would also be permanently reunited with his lost daughter. Or he could return to his wife, family, friends, and job. He asks, "Is what I do back home important? Does it matter? I really don't do much other than working and caring for my family and friends." Sarayu [the Holy Spirit figure] interrupts him. "Mack, if anything matters then everything matters. Because you are important, everything you do is important. Every time you forgive, the universe changes; every time you reach out and touch a heart or a life, the world changes; with every kindness and service, seen or unseen, my purposes are accomplished and nothing will ever be the same again."[108]

Centering prayer opens us to profound growth in love for others. By increasing our awareness of the present and thus opening us to the life flowing all around us, we can begin to live more profound lives as ambassadors of God's abundance to each person we meet each day.

CHAPTER 20

Freedom to Love

"Our hearts expand, overflowing with compassion
as we see the world through God's eyes of love.
We can act, rather than react, with greater purpose toward justice,
mercy, and healing in Jesus's name."

—AMY ODEN[109]

It is an error to associate the practice of centering prayer with a focus on God to the exclusion of other people. Silent meditative prayer is not an escape *from* others. It is an escape *for* others. The experience of the love of God manifests in a love for our neighbors. As Merton wrote, "Go into the desert not to escape other men but in order to find them in God."[110]

Centering prayer impacts the second core command of Scripture: Love your neighbor as yourself. As we've seen, there are actually two loves in view here: a love for others and a love for self.

Scripture as a whole refuses to separate our relationship with God from how we treat and relate with other people. In fact, the love of God moves us toward others. This is simply the way that God made us and the world. To be truly human is to be in relationship with God and others. Most of us understand this truth at the intellectual level, but on the ground, we face struggles.

Growth in Love

Sometimes those who seem to love others the best do so out of an inner brokenness. This may be seen in two contrasting ways. Many of us struggle with issues of codependence.[111] Codependence involves not merely putting the needs of another before our own, but in losing our identity in the other's neediness. Ironically, this type of behavior will often be reinforced in spiritual communities by praising the codependent person for their humility and service. But when we substitute codependence for authentic love we ironically grow in bitterness, and slowly the other becomes a project that we manage through a veneer of "love" rather than a person with whom we enjoy an authentic relationship in love.

An overcompensation to codependency is the practice of paternalistic or patronizing actions toward another. In the pursuit of holiness, there can be a subtle temptation to exalt oneself over those whom we serve. We, who are farther along the journey, can turn others into objects with whom we interact as their spiritual superiors. Often mentoring relationships utilize this type of power dynamics.

Even in works of service, there are people who we keep at arm's length as we hide behind titles, positions, and class. We see this illustrated most easily in short-term mission trips. We travel either to the "other side" of town or to a majority-world country to help "them." The assumption (often an unconscious one) is that we have something that they need. That we've been blessed more by God, so we are there to give back and show them the way. Not only are we wrong to approach ministry this way, but such relationships tend to be one-way transactions, not love.

Loving Free

As I've sat in silence before God, I've seen clearly my struggles with loving others. The root of this is suppressed anger and growing up a "nice guy." On top of this, misinterpretations of certain passages of Scripture created the false impression that a mark of true spirituality is not becoming angry. I understood the ideal of a Christian as someone who never offends, never expresses a negative thought, and never loses control.

For me the message of the cross turned into an excuse to not learn about proper boundaries in life. I tried to keep my cool at all times because I thought that this was what following Jesus meant. I sacrificed my right to be angry. In practice, I became a people pleaser. I tolerated the demands of others because I wanted to be liked. I kept the peace in difficult relationships by surrendering my opinions. I avoided having hard conversations at work, with friends, or with colleagues as I associated the feelings of tension and conflict with being "unchristian." Instead, I tried to bury my anger deep inside. It would appear occasionally as an outburst, perhaps in reaction to another's bad driving or in engaging in some passive-aggressive behavior.

Practicing centering prayer brought to my attention people in my life who caused me pain and hurt. In my thoughts, I reengaged people from my past whose actions still left bitter memories. I found myself reliving past moments. I even found myself rehashing old arguments. But I slowly learned to release these thoughts and recentered using my sacred word. This deliberate surrender has been healing. Over time it has become easier to surrender the past while in prayer.

As deep trust for God increases, our ability to release painful thoughts and feelings grows. Our love for God flows into our love for others. When this happens, your life expands because love is infinite. I can testify to this inner transformation.

CHAPTER 21

Free to Forgive

"And forgive us our debts, as we also have forgiven our debtors."
—MATTHEW 6:12

Forgiveness is the crucial lubricant of human

relationships. Mother Teresa connected loving compassion with
forgiveness when she wrote, "We must make our homes centers
of compassion and forgive endlessly."

This is an actionable item when we emerge from centering
prayer. Take a few moments and ponder persons who arose in
your thoughts. Do you recall any that you need to forgive? What
is stopping you now from releasing the offense? How would you
describe your feelings about the other?

The first critical response for loving neighbor is the practice
of forgiveness. Forgiveness sits at the center of the Lord's prayer.
We pray, "Forgive us our debts, as we also have forgiven our
debtors" (Matt. 6:12). This is the only action that Jesus's prayer
specifically assumes is true for those who pray it. It is the only
aspect of the prayer that is within our control. Scripture assumes
an inner awareness among believers of the need for forgiveness
and reconciliation.

For example, in Matthew 5:21–26, Jesus teaches of the need
for reconciliation. In fact, before offering a gift at the altar, a
worshiper should seek reconciliation with another brother or
sister who has something against him or her. Matthew 18:15–20
establishes a restorative process for resolving conflicts between

members. This is a core aspect of Matthew's teaching for the community of faith.

This is anchored by one of Jesus's most memorable parables: "The Parable of the Unforgiving Servant" (Matt. 18:21–35). Jesus begins by addressing a question from Peter. Peter asks Jesus if he should forgive an offending Christian as many as seven times. Peter believes he is showing genuine generosity. Jesus changes the paradigm with his shocking response, "Not seven times but seventy-seven times."

In other words, Jesus advocates unlimited forgiveness. Jesus goes on to illustrate the need for radical depths of forgiveness by telling of a king who forgives a servant of an immense and unpayable debt. Yet upon leaving the king's presence, the servant spies a fellow servant who owes about a day's wage. The servant has this man thrown into prison for this debt. The king hears about this incident and revokes the original debt forgiveness. The servant is then handed over for punishment. Jesus brings home the point in verse 35: "So my heavenly Father will also do to every one of you, if you do not forgive your brother or sister from your heart."

Jesus's words are serious, but his statement is not meant to cause us to forgive out of a fear of God's judgment. Instead, Jesus highlights the important role of forgiveness for embodying a life of love. If we cannot learn to forgive, we will find it difficult to give or receive love from others. It's that simple. The irony of a heart hardened against forgiving another is that we actually damage ourselves. Lewis Smedes wrote, "To forgive is to set a prisoner free and discover the prisoner was you."[112]

However, *forgiveness does not mean that we minimize the pain that the actions of another created in our life or in the lives of those whom we love.*

To forgive another is not an act against ourselves. It is not an admission that "it's all good." It is not an act of revictimization or humiliation. It definitely does not imply that we must continue to allow ourselves to be mistreated by others. It also does not automatically guarantee a full reconciliation with the people who hurt us. Reconciliation involves two parties. Forgiveness opens up the possibility of reconciliation, but it does not necessitate it. There is evil in this world that one should avoid.

Forgiveness is a spiritual act in which we consciously refuse to allow another's action to bind us to the past. The life of love is lived in the present moment. When we forgive as Jesus commands, we release junk that weighs us down. To move forward from past pain, we need to unclog our inner being.

What happens when we refuse to forgive? Forgiveness can be difficult because our false self enjoys its status as the aggrieved victim. It holds tight to grudges, old wounds, and memories of past hurts. For some of us these become badges of honor. Our victimhood becomes our identity. Yet past hurts only serve as anchors that prevent us from growing in love in the present. When we refuse to release our past pain, we stifle the development of our true self. Our inner world becomes a storehouse of dusty and unused junk that takes up space that otherwise God could fill with love. When we forgive, we clear out our inner storehouses, say "no" to our false self, and open our storehouses for new good things.

Centering prayer helps to facilitate the process. Images of persons and feelings of our deepest wounds will arise as we sit in silence. These are gentle nudges from our unconscious of blocks that we have to our spiritual growth. Our encounter with God in contemplation can slowly break up these deep-seated wounds. When these thoughts arise, we gently return to the true lover of our souls with our prayer word. In these moments, we are surrendering our memories of pain so that we can be *present in the moment to experience God with us.* These precious seconds slowly drain our past of its sting and facilitate in us the transformation into persons who can release our hurt and shame.

Reconciling Forgiveness

I want to return to Jesus's teaching from Matthew 18:15–35 one last time.

Much of what I've written focuses on our perspective as the one who needs to forgive. Jesus's words call us to extend forgiveness to others. Forgiveness is the healing balm of community. I've tried to make it clear that forgiveness and reconciliation are not always identical. However, they are dual goals when possible. L. Gregory Jones, in his rich study *Embodying Forgiveness: A Theological Analysis,* adopts the helpful term "reconciling forgiveness."[113] Reconciliation is vital because the life of love that God desires is inherently communal. This was true from the opening pages of Scripture.

Centering prayer helps us to break down the strongholds and walls that we've built up in response to deep pain and anger. When we release the roots of our hurt and rage, the capacity for forgiveness will slowly manifest. In silence before God, I discovered the faces of many persons from the past whose actions had created an inner prison of bitterness that I was holding onto. By God's grace, I released the grip that these old wounds had on my soul.

CHAPTER 22

The Power of Presence for Others

"If I am not in touch with my own belovedness,
then I cannot touch the sacredness of others."
—BRENNAN MANNING[114]

Since I've been sitting in silence with God,

I've learned to feel, observe, and release painful emotions. Learning to not react positively or negatively to images, thoughts, and memories while in prayer translates to my life. I can see this now in something as simple as driving. Traffic in Orlando is often intense compared with driving, say, in the Midwest or the rural Southeast. The Orlando roadways can be chaotic. In my recent past, observing dangerous driving (tailgating, aggressive merging) created anxiety and often anger in me. Lately I've noticed that, though I still sense a moment of anxiety, I release it along with any need to judge the other driver. Like many Americans, I spend a fair amount of time driving. This release of tension helps me to love my fellow drivers more than I have previously.

Recovery groups use the acronym "Halt" to be mindful of triggers and conditions. In fact, *halt* has its roots in a healing story of Jesus.

In John 5:3, Jesus finds a number of persons lying around a pool in Jerusalem called "Beth-zatha." The old King James describes these persons as "blind, halt, withered." The word *halt* means "lame" or "crippled." Bob Tuttle suggested to me once that we should view all people as halt. For our purposes, halt stands for hurt, angry, lonely, and tired. To see others through such a lens changes our perspective on the world. When we see others as potentially hurt, angry, lonely, and/or tired, we will respond to them differently.

Halt also opens up the possibility of showing kindness to self. We cannot be at our best all of the time. There are days of struggle. We will often feel hurt, angry, lonely, and tired. As we recognize pain in our lives, we gain perspective in relationship to the pain of others. We move from judges to ambassadors of God's abundance.

Letting Go of Judgment

We find ourselves attentive and open to another human being as our false self loses its seat of judgment. What does this look like? I've spent too much of my life inattentive to others because I was too focused on crafting my response. The truth of the matter was that I was more interested in my agenda than in the other.

But we get better. I remember sitting in an important business meeting a few years ago. I was serving as a consultant and was presenting a proposal to the leadership of the organization. After I made my presentation, one of the most vocal managers on the team challenged one of my proposed action items. This person often did this in meetings. Her behavior often intimidated others and shut down healthy debate. As she spoke, I can remember simply taking a few breaths and listening intently without judgment. I disagreed with her words, but I felt peace and calm in the moment. I was able to experience the moment as an observer. I could sense part of myself feeling slighted, a little embarrassed, and wanting to go on the defense. But I didn't. I released those thoughts and feelings. I remained present. In other words, I was able to refrain from reacting haphazardly or emotionally. After she finished speaking, I could sense others in the room (the entire management team was in attendance) turning their gaze toward me. I was fully present, so the time seemed to flow in slow motion. Before I could speak, the CEO answered the objection in support of my proposal. I didn't have to say a word. By not reacting emotionally or defensively, I opened up the opportunity for others to respond.

After the meeting, a key member of the leadership approached with a grin on her face and asked in jest, "What are you smoking? How did you do that?"

I don't want to give the impression that this always happens. I still lose myself in thought. I continue to assume a defensive posture more than I should. I remain an outstanding judge. People can still get under my skin as I take their words and actions personally. But slowly and steadily, I'm seeing the world differently. It's not that others have changed; I've changed. I'm listening to others more carefully now as an observer and curious learner rather than as judge and jury. In the process, I believe that I am growing in love for others.

CONCLUSION

As I look back over the journey that I've shared with you, I am filled with gratitude for the work that God has done in my life and continues to do by his grace. When I think back to where I was on that spring day almost a decade ago that I described in the introduction, I sit here amazed. I was surprised by the silence. Even more through the silence I was surprised anew by the love of the One who made me and who loves me.

I want to thank you for the privilege of sharing my experience and understanding of centering prayer with you. My prayer is that you have gained insight into the practice and the possibilities of centering prayer. Most importantly, I hope that you've already started a new practice or enhanced your existing one by reading my words.

Why not set a timer for twenty minutes and experience a time with the Lord now?

Set your intention to sit in silence with God. Open yourself to God's grace.

Close your eyes. Every time you find yourself lost in a thought simply recite your prayer word and return to the silence.

Remember the Four Rs:

Resist no thought.
Retain no thought.
React to no thought.
Return ever so gently to the sacred word.

Why not take the next step on your personal journey to love? But be careful—it may just change your life!

NOTES

1 Paul Tillich, *The Shaking of the Foundations* (New York: Charles Scribner's Sons, 1948), 161–162.

2 James C. Wilhoit, "Contemplative and Centering Prayer," *Journal of Spiritual Formation & Soul Care* 7.1 (2014), 109.

3 Although centering prayer is most often a solitary activity, participating in a group centering prayer environment is a moving experience. I've experienced group retreat settings. I also regularly invite students to join me before class for centering prayer.

4 Cynthia Bourgeault, *The Heart of Centering Prayer: Nondual Christianity in Theory and Practice* (Boulder, CO: Shambhala, 2016), 128.

5 Bourgeault, *The Heart of Centering Prayer*, 129. On 130, Bourgeault further describes "objectless awareness": "In the nano-second between the cessation of one thought and the arising of the next, there is a moment of pure consciousness where the subject and the object poles drop out and you're simply *there*. For a nanosecond, there's no 'you' and no God. No experience and no experiencer. There's simply a direct, undivided, sensate awareness of a single, unified field of being perceived from a far deeper place of aliveness. What is first tasted in a nanosecond can indeed become a stable and integrated state."

6 Alan Jones, *Soul Making: The Desert Way of Spirituality* (San Francisco: HarperCollins, 1989), 69.

7 Various translations of the *Cloud* exist. For this study I used William Johnston (ed.), *The Cloud of Unknowing and the Book of Privy Counseling* (New York: Image Books, 1996). This text is not an easy read. I recommend, however, examining at least chapters 3 and 5 (40–41, 45–46).

8 Bourgeault, *The Heart of Centering Prayer*, 117.

9 *The Cloud of Unknowing*, 40–41.

10 *The Cloud of Unknowing*, 45.

11 Thomas Keating, *Open Mind Open Heart: The Contemplative Dimension of the Gospel* (New York: Continuum Publishing, 2001), 73–74.

12 Eugene Yotka, "Centering Prayer and the Practice of Spiritual Direction," 5. This quotation is from a workbook used at The Awakening Institute during a Centering Prayer workshop on June 20, 2019.

13 Cynthia Bourgeault, *Centering Prayer and Inner Awakening* (Cambridge, MA: Crowley Publications, 2004), 17–18.

14 Murchadh Ó Madagáin, *Centering Prayer and the Healing of the Unconscious* (New York: Lantern Books, 2007), 42.

15 Bourgeault, *The Heart of Centering Prayer*, 32.

16 Thomas Merton, *New Seeds of Contemplation* (New York: New Directions, 1961), 39.

17 Edward Schillebeeckx, *The Church and Mankind* (New York: Seabury Press, 1976), 118.

18 See James Hollis, *Swamplands of the Soul: New Life in Dismal Places* (Toronto: Inner City Books, 1996), 11 and 61; and *The Middle Passage: From Misery to Meaning in Midlife* (Toronto: Inner City Books, 1993), 101–102. The language of true self, false self, and the shadow draws on psychoanalytic language. I will talk about these concepts in depth in Part 4. I merely introduce the ideas here as part of my discussion of the critical role that silence and solitude plays.

19 Hollis, *The Middle Passage*, 103.

20 Friedrich Nietzsche, *The Portable Nietzsche*, ed. and trans. Walter Kaufmann (New York: Penguin, 1977), 164.

21 Aleksandr I. Solzenitsyn, *The Gulag Archipelago Abridged: An Experiment in Literary Investigation* (New York: HarperPerennial, 2007), 75.

22 Bourgeault, *The Heart of Centering Prayer*, 17–19.

23 Richard Rohr, *The Naked Now: Learning to See as the Mystics See* (New York: Crossroad, 2009), 87.

24 Rohr, *The Naked Now*, 54. Read this quotation carefully. Rohr is not equating silence with God but reminding us that silence is not an indication of God's absence. In fact, God is often encountered in the silence. Recall Elijah's experience in 1 Kings 19:12.

25 Peter Rollins, *The Fidelity of Betrayal: Towards a Church Beyond Belief* (Brewster, MA: Paraclete Press, 2008), 92.

26 James Olthuis, *The Beautiful Risk: A New Psychology of Loving and Being Loved* (Eugene, OR: Wipf and Stock, 2006), 44.

27 Roberta C. Bondi, *To Love as God Loves: Conversations with the Early Church* (Philadelphia: Fortress, 1987), 17.

28 See Matthew 5:45, 48; 6:1, 4, 6, 8, 9, 14, 15, 18, 26, 32; and 7:11.

29 Bondi, *To Love as God Loves*, 18.

30 Bondi, *To Love as God Loves*, 23.

31 Quoted by Bondi, *To Love as God Loves*, 23. From Gregory of Nyssa's "On Perfection" in *Gregory of Nyssa: Ascetical Works*, trans. V. W. Callahan (Washington, DC: Catholic University of America Press, 1967), 122.

32 Tim Ferriss notes the high frequency of TM practitioners within his sample in *Tool of Titans: the Tactics, Habits, and Routines of Billionaires, Icons, and World-Class Performers* (New York: Houghton Mifflin Harcourt, 2017), 149–153.

33 Cynthia Bourgeault, "Centering Prayer and Radical Consent," *Sewanee Theological Review* 40.1 (1996) p. 47. See Sam Harris, *Waking Up: A Guide to Spirituality Without Religion* (New York: Simon & Schuster, 2014), 119–150.

34 Bourgeault, "Centering Prayer and Radical Consent," 48.

35 Amy Oden, *Right Here Right Now: The Practice of Christian Mindfulness* (Nashville: Abingdon, 2017), 96.

36 Wilhoit, "Contemplative and Centering Prayer," 116.

37 Bourgeault, "Centering Prayer and Radical Consent," 48–51. She acknowledges the influence of Gerald G. May's study *Will and Spirit: A Contemplative Psychology* (San Francisco: Harper and Row, 1982).

38 Cassian, John, *Conferences*, trans. Colm Luibheid (Mahwah, NJ: Paulist Press, 1985), 133. Quoted in Bourgeault, "Centering Prayer and Attention of the Heart," *Crosscurrents* 59 (1), 21.

39 Waldemar Janzen, *Exodus: Believers Bible Commentary* (Waterloo, ON: Herald Press, 2000), 258.

40 Bourgeault, "Centering Prayer and Radical Consent," 52.

41 Bourgeault, "Centering Prayer and Attention of the Heart," 21.

42 Bourgeault, "Centering Prayer and Attention of the Heart," 25–26.

43 Merton, *New Seeds of Contemplation*, 46.

44 Keith Ellis, *The Magic Lamp: Goal Setting for People Who Hate Setting Goals*, revised ed. (New York: Three Rivers, 1998), 74.

45 I was first introduced to this concept by Dr. David Seamands in his course "Servant as Pastoral Caregiver" (Spring 1992) at Asbury Theological Seminary. For a helpful and expanded discussion of this idea, see the classic work of J. B. Phillips, *Your God Is Too Small: A Guide for Skeptics and Believers Alike* (New York: Touchstone, 2004).

46 For example, see the recent best-selling work of Gabrielle Bernstein, *The Universe has Your Back: How to Turn Fear into Faith*, 2nd edition (Carlsbad, CA: Hay House, 2018). Or, reflect on the role of the "force" from the *Star Wars* movies.

47 Jonathan Edwards, *The Works of President Edwards*, Vol. 6 (New York: Burt Franklin, 1968), 461–62.

48 Merton, *New Seeds of Contemplation*, 15.

49 Roberta Bondi, *To Love as God Loves* (Philadelphia: Fortress, 1987), 23.

50 Cf. Mark 12:29–31, Luke 10:27.

51 Translation is my own based on Walter Moberly's exegesis of Deuteronomy 6:4 in which he argues for the translation "one and only" rather than the more common "alone" or "is one." See *Old Testament Theology: Reading the Hebrew Bible as Christian Scripture* (Grand Rapids, MI: Baker Academic, 2015), 18–20.

52 *The Apostolic Fathers I*, trans. Kirsopp Lake, The Loeb Classical Library (Cambridge, MA: Harvard University, 1912), 309.

53 See David G. Brenner's brief volume *The Gift of Being Yourself: The Sacred Call to Self-Discovery* (Downers Grove, IL: InterVarsity, 2004).

54 Bernard of Clairvaux, *On Loving God*, trans. Robert Walton; Cistercian Fathers, 13; (Kalamazoo, MI: Cistercian Publications, 1995).

55 Bernard of Clairvaux, *Honey and Salt: Selected Spiritual Writings of Saint Bernard of Clairvaux*, eds. John F. Thornton and Susan B. Varenne (New York: Vintage, 2007), 45.

56 Merton, *New Seeds of Contemplation*, 45.

57 Belden Lane, "Caring and Not Caring: The Desert Christians on Apathy," *The Christian Century* 127.10 (2010), 28.

58 *Open Mind, Open Heart*, 81–113. He includes a helpful summary of these
    categories on 111–113. Also see work of M. Basil Pennington, *Centering
    Prayer: Renewing an Ancient Christian Prayer Form* (Garden City, NY: Doubleday,
    1980), 80–84. Pennington covers the same essential territory but uses
    different terminology: (1) The Simple Thought, (2) The Catching Thought,
    (3) The Monitor, (4) The Bright Idea, and (5) Stressful Thoughts.

59 Pennington, *Centering Prayer*, 81.

60 Carl Arico, *A Taste of Silence: A Guide to the Fundamentals of Centering Prayer* (New
    York: Continuum, 1999), 132.

61 Pennington, *Centering Prayer*, 81.

62 Pennington, *Centering Prayer*, 103.

63 Pennington, *Centering Prayer*, 104.

64 Keating, *Open Mind, Open Heart*, 93.

65 The use of "demons" in this context is metaphorical. I'm not suggesting any
    type of literal exorcism. In *Right Here, Right Now*, Oden includes a section that
    warns about the disruptions that contemplative practices bring into our lives.
    See 93–95.

66 For an outstanding survey that traces *apatheia* from its development in Stoic
    thought to its use in Christian theology, see Joseph H. Nguyen, *Apatheia in the
    Christian Tradition: An Ancient Spirituality and Its Contemporary Relevance* (Eugene,
    OR: Wipf and Stock, 2018).

67 Simon Tugwell, "Evagrius and Macarius" in *The Study of Spirituality*, eds.
    Cheslyn Jones, Geoffrey Wainwright, and Edward Yarnold, SJ (New York:
    Oxford University Press, 1986), 171–72.

68 Belden Lane, "Caring and Not Caring: The Desert Christians on Apathy,"
    The Christian Century 127.10 (2010), 26.

69 Julia Konstantinovsky, "Evagrius Ponticus on Being Good in God and
    Christ," *Studies in Christian Ethics* 26.3 (2013), 323–26.

70 Thomas Merton, *Contemplative Prayer* (New York: Image, 1969), 4.

71 Evagrius's list of eight types of thoughts (see the following paragraphs) served
    as the inspiration for John Cassian's seven deadly sins. See Simon Tugwell,
    "Evagrius and Macarius" in *The Study of Spirituality*, 168–173, esp. 171. For
    those interested in other spiritual formation tools, Evagrius was influential in
    the development of what has become known as the enneagram. His list of
    "distracting thoughts" remains part of the spiritual direction that is possible
    with the enneagram. See Richard Rohr and Andreas Ebert, *The Enneagram: A
    Christian Perspective* (New York: Crossroad Publishing, 2001), 9–14.

72 John Eudes Bamberger, *Evagrius Ponticus: Praktikos and Chapters on Prayer*,
    Introduction, translation and notes by John E. Bamerger (Kalamazoo, MI:
    Cistercian Publications, 1981), 57, 62.

73 *Evagrius Ponticus*, 16–17.

74 Joseph Nguyen, *Apatheia in the Christian Tradition: An Ancient Spirituality and Its
    Contemporary Relevance* (Cascade, OR: Wipf and Stock, 2018), 25.

75 Nguyen, *Apatheia in the Christian Tradition*, 66–68. In his study, Nguyen traces
    the word "apatheia" back to its roots in Stoic philosophy and then shows how

Christian thinkers appropriated the term into Christian ethics and formation. For the Stoics, apatheia was the opposite of "excessive emotion." Christian theologians replaced the idea of excessive emotions with the "passions."

76 For those not familiar with the term "theology of the body" see Beth Felker-Jones, *Faithful: A Theology of Sex* (Grand Rapids, MI: Zondervan, 2015).

77 Ó Madagáin, *Centering Prayer and the Healing of the Unconscious*, 55–56.

78 Bondi, *To Love as God Loves*, 73–74.

79 Quoted in Tobon, "Apatheia in the Teaching of Evagrius Ponticus," 116. From Evagrius Ponticus, *The Monk: A Treatise on the Practical Life* in *Evagrius of Pontus: The Greek Ascetic Corpus*, ed. R. E. Sinkewicz (New York: Oxford University, 2003), 100.

80 Rohr, *Immortal Diamond: The Search for Our True Self* (San Francisco: Jossey-Bass, 2013), 29.

81 Thomas Keating. *Divine Therapy and Addiction: Centering Prayer and the Twelve Steps* (New York: Lantern Books, 2011).

82 Gustave Reininger, "Centering Prayer and the Christian Contemplative Tradition," in *Centering Prayer in Daily Life and Ministry* (New York: Continuum, 1998), 40.

83 Henri J. M. Nouwen, *Life of the Beloved: Spiritual Living in a Secular World* (New York: Crossroad, 2002).

84 Italics were used in the original. James K. A. Smith, *You are What You Love: The Spiritual Power of Habit* (Grand Rapids, MI: Brazos, 2016), 2.

85 Smith, *You are What You Love*, 32–38.

86 Keating equates the false self with Paul's *sarx*. See Thomas Keating, *Invitation to Love* (New York: Bloomsbury, 2012), 13.

87 Rohr, *Falling Upward: A Spirituality for the Two Halves of Life* (San Francisco: Jossey-Bass, 2011), 46.

88 Macrina Wiederkehr, *Seven Sacred Pauses: Living Mindfully Through the Hours of the Day* (Notre Dame: Ave Maria, 2008), 178.

89 Rohr, *Falling Upward*, 51.

90 Cynthia Bourgeault, "Centering Prayer and Attention of the Heart," 16.

91 Henri Nouwen, *The Prayer of the Heart* (New York: Ballantine, 2003), 15.

92 Evan Howard, *A Guide to Christian Spiritual Formation: How Scripture, Spirit, Community, and Mission Shape Our Souls* (Baker Academic, 2018), 31–32 and 34–38.

93 Keating, *Invitation to Love*, 14–15. See 17–22 for Keating's personal illustration of the struggle.

94 Gerald May, *Addiction and Grace* (San Francisco: HarperCollins, 1988), 168.

95 Rohr, *Falling Upward*, 61–62.

96 See Brendan Manning, *Abba's Child: The Cry of the Heart for Intimate Belonging* (Colorado Springs: NavPress, 2015), 11. Calvin affirms Augustine's reading. See Calvin's *Commentary on Romans*, https://ccel.org/ccel/calvin/calcom38/calcom38.xii.ix.html.

97 Rohr, *The Naked Now*, 141.

98 Rohr, *The Naked Now*, 15.

99 Rohr, *The Naked Now*, 127.

100 From "And Can It Be That I Should Gain," Charles Wesley, 1738.

101 Thomas Merton. *The Sign of Jonas* (New York: Harcourt Brace, 1953), 261.

102 Erwin Raphael McManus, *An Unstoppable Force: Daring to Become the Church God Had in Mind* (Loveland, CO: Group, 2001), 148.

103 Thomas Keating, "The Practice of Attention/Intention" in *Centering Prayer in Daily Life and Ministry*, ed. Gustave Reininger (New York: Continuum International, 1997), 13–19.

104 See Brother Lawrence, *Practice of the Presence of God*, "Fourth Conversation," https://www.ccel.org/ccel/lawrence/practice.iii.iv.html.

105 Keating, "The Practice of Attention/Intention" in *Centering Prayer in Daily Life and Ministry*, 18.

106 Steve Payne, "The Tradition of Prayer in Teresa and John of the Cross," in *Spiritual Traditions for the Contemporary Church*, eds. Robin Maas and Gabriel O'Donnell (Nashville: Abingdon, 1990), 246–47.

107 Dietrich Bonhoeffer, *Life Together*, trans. and Introduction by John W. Doberstein (San Francisco, HarperSanFrancisco, 1954), 99. This reflection on practical ministry follows an entire chapter on the disciplines of solitude and silence (see 76–89).

108 William P. Young, *The Shack* (Newbury Park, CA: Windblown Media, 2007), 235.

109 Amy Oden, *Right Here Right Now* (Nashville: Abingdon, 2017), 22.

110 Merton, *New Seeds of Contemplation* (New York: New Directions Books, 1962), 53.

111 Tim Clinton and Gary Sibcy, *Attachments: Why You Love, Feel, and Act the Way You Do* (Nashville: Thomas Nelson, 2019).

112 Lewis B. Smedes, *Forgive and Forget: Healing the Hurts We Don't Deserve* (San Francisco: HarperOne, 1996), 133.

113 L. Gregory Jones, *Embodying Forgiveness: A Theological Analysis* (Grand Rapids, MI: Eerdmans, 1995). See especially 182–197.

114 Manning, *Abba's Child*, 39.

ACKNOWLEDGMENTS

The writing of this book has been one of the best experiences of my life. After my life turned upside down about a decade ago, contemplative spiritual practices restored the vitality of my faith and infused my life with love and deep joy. The practice of centering prayer continues to sit at the center of my daily rhythms. I stumbled into centering prayer, and this book is the story of my practice. This manuscript started as a random collection of thoughts and reflections on my experiences and my slow rebirth into the person that I am today. I am grateful that it grew into the book that you hold in your hands.

I want to thank Jon Sweeney and Paraclete Press for their support in bringing my book idea to a wider audience. I am truly appreciative for the Paraclete team's enthusiasm and willingness to support a Bible professor's venture into the world of spiritual formation.

Thank you to my dear friend of almost thirty years Dr. Mike Voigts (and now colleague at Asbury Seminary). He supported me during the darkest days of my journey and has always been a generous friend. He read two drafts of my manuscript and gave wise counsel to me. He also first introduced me to the writings of Bernard of Clairvaux and Thomas Merton.

Thank you to my colleagues Dr. Steve Stratton and Dr. Toddy Holeman as well as Reverend Eugene Yotka for our monthly conversations about centering prayer and contemplative spirituality. I've learned much from them. Special thanks to Steve for first introducing me to centering prayer through the work of Thomas Keating and gifting me with Ó Madagáin's *Centering Prayer and the Healing of the Unconscious* and to Gene, who was my formal teacher in centering prayer through a workshop at his Awakening Institute in Cocoa, Florida.

Thank you to Dr. Steve Harper for reading a draft of this manuscript and encouraging me to publish it. It was Steve who first suggested Paraclete Press.

I'm grateful for my friends at the First United Methodist Church in Winter Park. I presented a brief introduction to centering prayer and lectio divina there in 2018 when I was beginning the writing process. Their support and enthusiasm encouraged me to keep going. Grady McClendon, a long-term member of the congregation and my friend, took an interest in the project and read a draft in early 2020. His editorial eye helped me to write with greater clarity.

I'm grateful for feedback on earlier drafts by former students of mine: Justin Systema, Keith Harcombe, David Collette, and Hector Nieves.

Thank you to all of my current students who show up early to class to sit in silent meditative prayer with me as preparation for our day of study.

Thank you to my daughters Micaela and Katrina. You saw your dad at his most anxious moments. I'm glad that you've witnessed and experienced my rebirth too!

Finally, my heart is full of love and gratitude for my wife and soul partner, Astrid. It has been pure joy building a life with you. Your calm, kind, and loving soul has enriched me and serves daily as a sure foundation for us to grow and experience love and life together.

ABOUT THE AUTHOR

Brian D. Russell, PhD, serves as a Professor of Biblical Studies at Asbury Theological Seminary in Orlando, Florida, and as a coach for pastors and spiritual leaders. He is available in person and virtually for speaking, retreats, one-on-one mentoring, and group coaching.

For more information, visit
www.deepdivespirituality.com.

Email Brian:

deepdivespirituality@gmail.com

Social Media:

You Tube Channel: Deep Dive Spirituality with Dr. Brian Russell
Twitter: @briandrussell
Instagram: @yourprofessorforlife

Podcast:

The Deep Dive Spirituality Conversations Podcast
www.deepdivespirituality.podbean.com/
Or search on your favorite source for podcasts.

ABOUT PARACLETE PRESS

PARACLETE PRESS is the publishing arm of the Cape Cod Benedictine community, the Community of Jesus. Presenting a full expression of Christian belief and practice, we reflect the ecumenical charism of the Community and its dedication to sacred music, the fine arts, and the written word.

Learn more about us at our website:
www.paracletepress.com
or phone us toll-free at 1.800.451.5006

SCAN
TO
READ
MORE

YOU MAY ALSO BE INTERESTED IN. . .

Be Still and Listen
Experience the Presence of God in Your Life
Amos Smith
Foreword by Phileena Heuertz,
Afterword by Dale Hanson Bourke

ISBN 978-1-61261-865-4
Trade paperback | $16.99

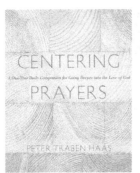

Centering Prayers
A One-Year Daily Companion for Going Deeper Into the Love of God
Peter Traban Haas

ISBN 978-1-61261-415-1
Trade paperback | $19.99

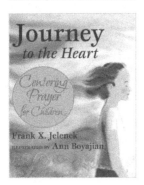

FOR CHILDREN
Journey to the Heart
Centering Prayer for Children
Frank Jelenek

ISBN 978-1-55725-482-5
Trade paperback | $18.99

Available at bookstores
Paraclete Press | 1-800-451-5006 | www.paracletepress.com